PRAISE FOR

FROM THE
BLOOD ᴼ̄ᶠ ABEL

"The Bible itself tells us to 'rightly divide the word of truth.' For 2000 years, Christians have divided the testaments, but following René Girard, Distefano argues that there are two streams within the Scriptures, one of religion and the other of God's revelation. *From the Blood of Abel* is a marvelous introduction to Girardian thought for any struggling Evangelical who is seeking the really good news of Christ Jesus."

—**Michael Hardin, executive director at Preaching Peace and author of *The Jesus Driven Life***

"Matthew Distefano offers us a robust and intriguing approach to the Gospel. Having had his Christianity restructured both by Girard's insights into violence, and by Becker's understanding of death, he makes available a much stronger and richer sense of what Jesus was about in undoing those things than so many approaches which pile quote upon quote, leaving readers at the mercy of their own violence. Those questioning received notions of hell, of wrath, and of an exclusive God will find solid food here."

—**James Alison, Catholic priest, theologian, and author**

"In this marvelous follow-up to *All Set Free*, Matthew Distefano synthesizes Girard's 'mimetic theory' and Becker's 'death anxiety' to diagnose the causes of human violence right to the roots. He then faithfully applies the Christ-solution as our effectual, life-giving remedy. It is especially striking that the author moves easily from theology and theory into real-life scenarios and testimonies. He recounts the excruciating reality of violence and exclusion—but does so to spotlight the power of the beautiful gospel."

—Brad Jersak, editor at *CWR Magazine*,
faculty at *Westminster Theological Centre*, and
author of *A More Christlike God: A More Beautiful Gospel*

"Matthew Distefano's *From the Blood of Abel* is a provocative examination of the problem of human violence through the lenses of mimetic theory and Christian theology. Distefano marshals theology, sociology, psychology, anthropology, philosophy, and history to lead readers through humanity's horrifically violent past and present, and challenges us to look more closely at the ultimate hope for peace that Christianity provides. Distilling insights from René Girard, Ernest Becker, and Michael Hardin, Distefano offers a vibrant and astute assessment of humanity's seemingly implacable violent tendencies and skillfully shows how the Bible effectively—and often surprisingly—addresses our most fundamental problem."

—Dan Wilkinson, editor of the
***Unfundamentalist Christians* blog on Patheos**

"Matthew Distefano's *From the Blood of Abel* is the book that our country and our world needs right now. In a day where Christians are known for our violent rhetoric, persecution complex, and scapegoating of all those who don't fit within our theological paradigm, Distefano powerfully speaks the truth of the Gospel of peace in an accessible and deeply moving way that will shatter the false images of God so many of us have been taught to believe in. In place of the false images, Distefano unveils that the face of God is revealed in Christ, a face that has the power to truly redeem our world. This book is a must read!"

—Brandan Robertson, author of
Nomad: A Spirituality for Travelling Light

"Matthew's desire to heal the human spirit is palpable in his writing. He rightly identifies the human problem of violence as a temporary means of relieving spiritual tension or uneasiness. Following the insights of René Girard, Matthew walks the reader through the many reasons we create, or become, victims of violence. Finding a solution to our collective problem leads the reader straight to the heart of Jesus. By the final chapter, Matthew passionately implores the reader to imitate the peaceful, forgiving image of God, modeled in the person of Jesus Christ. A good read for those who dare to hope for a better tomorrow."

—Carol Wimmer, author of *The Clock: A Timekeeping Tool for the Church of Tomorrow*

"Humanity has a problem, and that problem has a name. The only problem is that we've been largely unable to name this unseeable issue that seems to plague us from the moment we first throw a punch at our siblings for taking away our favorite toy. In many ways, the modern surge toward understanding our personal anthropology, and specifically that which is in relation to our own spirituality as well, has been not unlike a pressure-cooker, whistling and gaining volume until someone finally blows the lid off and releases the pressure. What comes out has such force its best to step back and watch from a distance. What is this problem? War, but more to the point, it is in our propensity toward war as a default response to social dissonance. Whether that is a war against metaphorical icons like terror or drugs, or war against other humans, we wage it whenever given the chance. In *From the Blood of Abel*, Matthew Distefano shows this in force, while making the necessary, important connection between the deity we worship, the theology we espouse, and the wars we wage in the temporal—all while remaining faithful to those serious students of Girardian philosophy and theology. Whether or not we will ever be free of the cancer that is human violence remains to be seen, but the more we have voices like Matthew's, flooding the scene with this truth, the greater hope I have for that end."

—Caleb Miller, author of *The Divine Reversal: Recovering the Vision of Jesus Christ as the Last Adam* and *Saving God: Freeing Abba from the Captivity of Religion*

"When reaching the final quarter of faith's pilgrimage in life, it's a natural instinct to look back to see if anyone is coming after one's self with the same spiritual heart beat. When I metaphorically look back, I rejoice to see a new generation of young theological thinkers (in their twenties and thirties) who have already grappled with issues that some of us did not come to grips with until our fifties or sixties... if ever! I truly feel a fatherly 'cheer' arise in my heart for them. Matthew Distefano is of that number.

Matthew's book, *From the Blood of Abel* is an excellent book to recommend to seekers who have begun to question traditional Evangelical teachings on alleged God-sanctioned violence, a sacrificial hermeneutic, doctrines of hell and eternal punishment, and much more. Matthew has processed weightier works on these topics and synthesized their salient points into a volume that is reachable to the majority who may have neither time nor inclination to read academic-level treatments on those subjects. In doing so, Matthew has done the body of Christ a great service. I wish I had read a book like *From the Blood of Abel* when I was twenty-one. If I had, my life would have charted a much different and much more Christ-conformed path, much earlier."

—Stephen R. Crosby, D. Min., founder of *Stephanos Ministries* and author of *How New is the New Covenant?* and 13 other titles

"If you have stayed away from the Bible because it's filled with violence and superstitious myths or because the God of the Bible seems violent, wrathful and prone to punishment, you may have overlooked a singular resource for peace. Matthew Distefano offers a persuasive case for reading Scripture as revealing two intertwined realities: humanity's violence and God's nonviolence. Making good use of the mimetic insight of René Girard, Distefano guides his readers gently but confidently to a new understanding of the unity between the Old and New Testaments, between the God of Abraham, Isaac, and Jacob and the God revealed by Jesus' death and resurrection. Distefano believes that the Bible contains God's plan for achieving peace in the here and now. When you have finished *From the Blood of Abel*, you will find yourself believing, too."

—Suzanne Ross, cofounder of *The Raven ReView* and author of *The Wicked Truth: When Good People Do Bad Things*

"Matthew Distefano's *From the Blood of Abel* is a literary construction of power, precision and depth perfectly positioned for such a time as this. Navigating through layers and angles of human history, psychology, and spirituality, Matthew tactfully backs the reader and all humanity into the corner—dissecting, diagnosing and disarming our intoxication with violence. One cannot help but to be changed and perhaps even a bit haunted by the revelation of this monumental writing."

—Chris Kratzer, pastor and blogger at chriskratzer.com

"Despite two centuries of exponential growth in human flourishing, our propensity for violence is still a fundamental theological issue. In *From the Blood of Abel*, Matthew Distefano does what few writers can do: he uses tools from multiple disciplines to unearth the origins of human conflict, yet still presents a hopeful path forward. Through biblical analysis and the insights of intellectual giants René Girard and Ernest Becker, Distefano shows how the answer to the human condition is the Gospel of Jesus Christ—the True Human. His argument is captivating and deserves the attention of all who care about resolving human conflict. Even those unconvinced by some of Distefano's conclusions will profit from his penetrating analysis of what ails the world and the God who heals it."

**—Doug Stuart, regular contributor
for *The Libertarian Christian Institute***

"Matthew Distefano's book, *From the Blood of Abel*, places bible stories in their historical context and in the light of modern anthropological insight, revealing an astonishing and refreshing depth of meaning. The book digs to the roots of who we are, and offers a view of Christianity that addresses our tendency to be separatists, sometimes to the point of violence. Much of the 'Christianity' we imagine postpones heaven to the postmortem, and rips humanity apart in the meantime. But Matthew reminds us that the kingdom of God is within us, and that Jesus doesn't heal this world through war, ethnic or religious cleansing, or the devaluation of the 'other'; but through forgiveness, reconciliation, and love."

**—Wendy Francisco, author and animator
of the book and viral video, *GoD and DoG***

FROM THE
BLOOD
OF ABEL

HUMANITY'S ROOT CAUSES OF VIOLENCE AND THE
BIBLE'S THEOLOGICAL-ANTHROPOLOGICAL SOLUTION

MATTHEW J. DISTEFANO

Copyright © 2016 by Matthew J. Distefano.

First Edition

Cover design and layout by Rafael Polendo (polendo.net)

Scripture quotations, unless otherwise noted, taken from the New Revised Standard Version and are copyright © 1989 by the Division of Christian Education of the National Council of Churches of Christ in the U.S.A. and are used by permission.

Scriptures taken from the Holy Bible, New International Version®, NIV®. Copyright ©1973, 1978, 1984, 2011 by Biblica, Inc.™ Used by permission of Zondervan. All rights reserved worldwide. www.zondervan.com The "NIV" and "New International Version" are trademarks registered in the United States Patent and Trademark Office by Biblica, Inc.™

Revised Standard Version of the Bible, copyright 1952 (2nd edition, 1971) by the Division of Christian Education of the National Council of the Churches of Christ in the United States of America. Used by permission. All rights reserved.

Chapter 1: Permission granted by Dominic Moes to use the testimony contained in his December 27, 2015 email to the author. Permission granted by Robert Lofgren to use the testimony contained in his August 7, 2016 email to the author.

Chapter 2: Permission granted by Brian Cordova to use the testimony contained in his April 2, 2016 email to the author. Permission granted by Suzanne Ross and The Raven ReView to use the content from the poster entitled "Mimetic Desire."

Chapter 5: Permission granted by Adam Ericksen to use the essay entitled "Myth and Gospel."

ISBN 978-1-938480-18-8

This volume is printed on acid free paper and meets ANSI Z39.48 standards. Printed in the United States of America

 QUOIR

Published by Quoir
Orange, California

www.quoir.com

DEDICATION

For Lyndsay and Elyse, Michael and Speri, and everyone from the 2015 and 2016 Making Peace Conferences

TABLE OF CONTENTS

FOREWORD

There are a handful of books that I wish I could travel back in time and give to the twenty years younger version of myself. After reading the one you are presently holding, I have added it to the list.

In my journey as a Christian, I have undergone many a struggle to maintain my faith. The younger, and more inexperienced I was, the fewer struggles I had, but the longer I lived, the more life's not-so-pleasant experiences became my own. And as hard as I tried to withstand their force, many of these experiences literally destroyed my Christianity, forcing me to rebuild the entire structure of my faith from the ground up.

My experience is in no way unique, but represents the path trodden by every honest soul, whether Christian, Jewish, Buddhist, Muslim, atheist, or any other designation of belief or unbelief we have come up with. For me, however, it was specifically my understanding of the Gospel, its God, and its Christ, that was shaken by my experiences of life. When I watched the Towers fall on 9/11, for example, as a first year ministry school student, it was something of the beginning of the end. My heart shattered within me, and I wept like I had never wept before. How could such awful suffering be visited upon innocent lives like this? How could anyone be as cruel and deluded as to think such an action would be pleasing to a god of any sort, and result in eternal bliss? So many questions. So few answers. But, the biggest question of all was how God could allow this? In my then-naivety (as if I have gotten over it), though, this was one question I did, in fact, manage to come up with an answer to: we were living in the last days, and such things simply had to occur to make way for "the end." I explained away this atrocity and all those that followed with the waving of this magic wand—and I waited, and waited, and waited—just as I had been doing since my early childhood. But, just like always, the violence continued, the questions remained unanswered, and that "last trump" I imagined would end all this senseless violence, and usher in eternal peace, remained unblown.

Eventually, this belief in a Jesus who would swoop in to rapture us off of a scorched earth, turn lions vegan, and enable children to play with cobras like kittens, failed me, and failed me hard. That is not to say I gave up hope in a God who will, to quote N.T. Wright, "set the world right once and for all,"[1] but that I had to let go of the notion that the Gospel's only solution to such violence was to call us to stare at the sky, and wait for God to take us away from it all. When the Towers fell, I thought only the rapture could follow. Instead, war was declared, resulting in what has been well over a decade of constant death and bloodshed, with no rapture in sight. This, along with the almost daily acts of terrorism and random acts of violence, all too quickly became our new normal. I decided that if my "gospel" could not handle it, because it could only offer me an escape, but no solution, then maybe it was not worth holding onto.

And so I decided to let go of it.

I was a pastor at the time, yet my faith simply became unsustainable. I could not cope with the dissonance being created by the clashing of my God-beliefs with the very real world in which I found myself. My "gospel" could say nothing to any of it. Nothing. Zilch. Nada. Sure, I could condemn the violence, the war, the bloodshed, but even those who I thought were on the wrong end of it were not safe in my worldview. Even the victims, if they were unbelievers, were burning in an eternal hell of my own God's making. I simply had no answer for any of it. As it turned out, the God whom I thought was the solution was just as bad as the other guy's god—and therefore just as much of a problem.

It all quickly ceased to make any sense, whatsoever. And so, as I said, I decided to let it go. For a season I took comfort in the more gracious forms of the faith I already held, but that did not work for long. I turned to atheistic philosophies and humanism, and while I consider that a valuable leg of my journey, I ultimately did not find what I was thirsting for there either. I felt lost and untethered from all that seemed safe, as though I were hurtling through space, with nothing sure to grab onto. Every now and again, in the name of finding some sacred solidity, I would look back longingly at the rubble that was once my robust faith, but because my experience with it had been so disappointing, it was the last thing I wanted to return to. Sometimes, though, in my more honest moments, I could hear the voice of something genuine, something true, something pure, calling to me from beneath all of the mess. And so I began to sift through it all. Inevitably, most of the rubble was just that—rubble—and I found nothing redeemable in about ninety-nine percent of it. When I got to the bottom of it all, though, I discovered the voice that had drawn me in the first place.

This "voice" I am speaking of is the figure of Jesus that I was initially captured by, but who had been mutated over the years by religion, and turned into something that looked nothing like the man we read of in the Gospels. I was reintroduced to this Jesus in the works of men like René Girard, Michael Hardin,

Walter Wink, and others whose approach to the Gospel actually made sense in light of a world like the one we find ourselves living in. As it turned out, it was never Jesus who failed me, just the layers and layers of tradition, religion, and dogma Christendom had encased him in. But beneath all of that was something that actually spoke to the condition of the world and actually provided solutions that went beyond the eschatological and the speculative. The voices of these theologians, anthropologists, and philosophers helped me to find this "voice," this Word, this Jesus, and ultimately, saved my faith.

That same voice is here, in Matthew Distefano's masterful work, *From the Blood of Abel*. This is precisely the sort of book I, as a struggling young pastor, desperately needed to have in my hands. I had to do the hard work of sifting through mounds of books on theology and anthropology that I could barely understand; all while being only inches away from losing interest and throwing the entire Christianity thing in the garbage. In order to retool my faith, and find a version of it that was actually livable in this world, I had to dig in and study in ways that many simply do not have the time or sometimes even the mental or spiritual strength to do. Had I been given a book like the one you are now holding, the whole process may have been a lot easier on a guy who did not even know what the word anthropology, let alone "mimesis" meant. Distefano manages to distill the sometimes complicated works of men like René Girard and Ernest Becker, into a very approachable, and easy to understand form—and then puts his own unique spin on it, so as to create something distinctive and potentially life-altering.

From his opening chapter on the problem of violence and the horrors of war, to his look at the Scriptures, the cross, and resurrection in light of a non-violent, forgiving God, to his closing thoughts on the love of God and humanity's final but glorious destination, Distefano has managed to create something that would have liberated the past me, but that captivated, moved, and inspired the present me.

While millions of Christians the world over are finding the Christianity they have inherited untenable in light of the world in which they live, there is a voice speaking loudly and clearly. While Christianity itself is quickly coming to be considered an outdated relic that belongs in the dustbin of history, alongside all other religions that have come before it, that voice speaks through prophets and writers like Distefano, who has managed to paint the Gospel in such a way that even an atheist could appreciate its beauty. The Gospel Distefano preaches is not one that simply promises evacuation, or posits posthumous rewards for those who endure the nastiness of the here and now. No, his Gospel speaks directly to the nastiness, exposes it for what it is, and then offers the solution in the person of Jesus. This is not a Gospel of rapture, or rewards and reprisals, but the good news of what God has done in history to stem the tide of our own evolution and violence, and that invites us into a whole new way of living and being in this world. The struggling evangelical and the unbeliever alike can take refuge here, finding in this message the thing their soul—and the world that seems to be crumbling all around them—is thirsting for.

–JEFF TURNER

PREFACE

While writing my first book, *All Set Free*, I had a bit of a chip on my shoulder. This was due in large part to the pain my years in the church caused me. And so, at times, I would catch myself becoming fixated on trying to defend my new doctrinal beliefs—i.e. universal reconciliation—against the naysayers, rather than simply putting forth an understanding of the Gospel with the sole intention of having it become a balm for healing. It is not that the book has failed to be that, because based on most of the feedback I have received it really has been. And for that I am reverentially grateful. However, looking back, perhaps my intentions were not always the purest. Self-reflection indicates this book is much different in this regard.

That being said, the idea for this project emerged from an essay that I published for *The Raven ReView* early in 2016, entitled "The Root of Violence: Imitative Desire, Death Anxiety, and the Gospel's Solution to Both."[1] Prior to the release, I made a comment on Twitter, notifying others about it, and one of my friends, J.J. Valenzuela, responded: "sounds more like a book… or tome…than an essay."[2] So I got to thinking: *You know what, this could be a book!* And roughly three weeks later, after beginning an introduction and sketching out a rough outline, *From the Blood of Abel* was born. So thank you, J.J., for ultimately being responsible for this book's genesis.

In reflecting upon the process of writing *From the Blood of Abel*, I have come to the stark realization of just how difficult it was to put together, both in terms of intellectual and emotional effort. First, unlike *All Set Free*, this book underwent a major rewrite per the recommendation of a friend and scholar, and I am glad it did because it turned out much tighter and cohesive. But it took a lot of work nonetheless. Emotionally, it was grueling due to the content it deals with. For an example, in the first chapter I confront the brutality of war and violence, and then the fallout due to the human propensity toward both. Researching statistics and reading through all of the first-hand accounts of terror— in order to snag just the right one—was absolutely exhausting. Actually, it was more than that. It was horrifying.

What madness we humans create!

My foray into the world of mayhem and death, then, has forced me to ponder my own demise. How can it not? I think of Ernest Becker's quote, where he reminds us how the Angel of Death is always on our shoulder, just waiting to "extend his wing."[3] Certain moments in life make you well aware of that Angel's wing, even as it begins to open ever so slightly: a near death experience, a poor prognosis from a physician, the death of a loved one, etc. Diving headfirst into this project has been one of those events. Surely, it is not as profound as something like a near death experience, but it has affected me in the same kind of way nonetheless.

Ultimately though, I live with the hope that no matter what happens—yes, even death—God will restore life. *All life!* In fact, this is a major theme throughout the second and third parts of the book. So while the first half is dedicated to the topic of violence and its underlying root causes and can be rather gruesome and tiring (and a bit didactical), we end our journey with hope. And in a world so torn up by violence, so wrecked by humanity's systems of death, if we have hope in a God of life, then we have enough.

ACKNOWLEDGMENTS

I would like to thank my wife, Lyndsay, for her continual support, and for being such a source of strength. Without her, I would feel as if I were nothing. She perpetually amazes me with her willingness to grow and to become a more loving person. My daughter and I are quite lucky to have her.

Thank you to my parents, Dave and Sharon, for their continual support throughout the years.

I have to thank my best friend, Mike Machuga, for everything...from late night talks on his back porch, to early morning hikes to the tops of some of California's greatest peaks, and now the latest, for coauthoring our forthcoming book, *A Journey with Two Mystics: Conversations between a Girardian and a Wattsian*.

My friends, Dominic Moes, Robert Lofgren, and Brian Cordova each contributed their stories in brief and for that, I must say "thank you." All three testimonies are very heartfelt and moving and required a lot of vulnerability, given the nature of each one's history. A hearty thank you to my friend and colleague Adam Ericksen (*The Raven ReView*), who contributed an essay that is, like all of his work, top-notch. And finally, thank you to the one and only Jeff Turner who wrote the magnificent foreword for this book. Again, I am afraid the forewords are the best parts of both of my first two books. But given how good each are, I am also okay with that.

I would like to thank all my other friends and colleagues at *The Raven ReView* for all that they do. To Lindsey: for editing all my articles and for her masterful review of *All Set Free*. To Suzanne: for teaching me more than she knows over this past year. And to Maura: for promoting all of the amazing work the "flock" produces.

I owe a debt of gratitude to all those folks who read an early copy of my manuscript and who offered wonderful insights and critiques. They include Carol Wimmer, Doug Stuart, Stephen Crosby, Dan Wilkinson, Michael Hardin, and Mark Stone. Also, I must offer a huge "thank you" to my primary editor, Mike DeVries, as well as my final editor Mark Hilditch, who both did fabulous jobs. The final copy would not nearly be what it is today without all of the help I received.

I also want to thank Michael Hardin for being such a great friend, and one helluva theological mentor. I am proud to be called "grasshopper."

To all those I have been fortunate enough to work and publish with, including *Wipf & Stock Publishers*, *Sojourners*, *ProgressiveChristianity.org*, *PreachingPeace.org*, *The Clarion Journal*, *Jesism.com*, *The New Reformers*, and *Unfundamentalist Christians* on "Patheos": thank you.

To everyone who was a part of "Making Peace" 2015 and 2016, thank you for changing my life. I will never forget those weeks in Pennsylvania.

Lastly, I want to thank everyone who has signed up for my blog at www.allsetfree.com, everyone who has donated money, everyone who has purchased my first book and who reads my articles, and everyone who spreads the word about the message of peace that I am attempting to deliver.

May God bless all of you!

INTRODUCTION

"Our wisdom, insofar as it ought to be deemed true and solid wisdom, consists of two parts: the knowledge of God and of ourselves. But as these are connected together by many ties, it is not easy to determine which of the two precedes and gives birth to the other."[1]

—JOHN CALVIN

I can hear my friends and avid readers now: "Matthew! You are beginning your Introduction with a Calvin quote?!" *Why, yes, yes I am.* And here is why: because, regardless of the many things I disagree with Calvin over, it is a great quote. Indeed, without knowing ourselves we cannot expect to know God and without knowing God we cannot truly know ourselves. The sad thing is this though: so many of us do not act as if this is true. We talk about God in terms of loftiness, like a king on his almighty white throne. God is omni-*everything*. And perhaps God is, but that is not really my point here. My point is that we then turn around and, in spite of humans being made in God's image, talk about ourselves as lowly "filthy rags," for instance (Isa 64:6). We treat others as such, too. We do things like insist, with chillingly cold faces, how those we do not like are going to burn in hell for their iniquities. Then we do our part to send them there through war and conquest and terror. Or, as Friedrich Nietzsche brilliantly wrote: "One must let oneself be misled: they say 'judge not!' but they sent to hell everything that stands in their way."[2]

And so, the first part of this book will attempt to address the reasons why we do this—in fact, why we have *always* been doing this. You see, violence is like a drug, an opiate we cannot get enough of. As Greek philosopher Heraclitus noted, "It is the structuring principle of reality."[3] So without it, we would lose a part of our "identity." Yet, because of it, we have made life a living hell for an innumerable number of people over the course of history. Certainly, we all acknowledge this to some degree.

But the real question is this: *What can be done about it?*

In the second part of this book, we will set out to discover an answer. And, as the subtitle suggests, we will turn to the Scriptures, both Hebrew and Christian alike. But we will have to be careful in how we handle these Scriptures, because depending on how you approach them, you can get them to say just about anything you want them to. For example, if you want to justify something horrific like slavery, you can. In fact, the first president of the South Carolina State Baptist Convention did just that, as late as 1838. He wrote, "The right of holding slaves is clearly established by the Holy Scriptures, both by precept and example."[4] With regard to violence in general, then, the Bible establishes a justification as well, also both by precept and example.

And this is my primary concern with a flat hermeneutic, or in other words, a literalist approach to Scripture. For you see, the Bible is a bloody book and I do not mean that in the way the British use "bloody"—as a noun intensifier, that is. Rather, what I mean is that if it were a movie, it would be rated R for the incessant use of divinely-mandated violence. Thematically, violence is front and center as warring clans constantly attempt to wipe each other off the face of the earth. From the great and mighty Pharaohs of Egypt and Caesars of Rome, all the way down to the smallest tribes of Judah, war was king and, to paraphrase the poet and prophet Bob Dylan, they waged it "with God on their side."[5] That includes the God of Israel, or in other words, the God of the Bible.

On the other hand, though, I cannot deny how the Bible, as if held in tension with itself, is also a book that testifies to the power of mercy, forgiveness, grace, and peace. Much of the perspective of the writers is not "from above," but rather "from below"—telling the stories of a once *enslaved* people, who are delivered from bondage by a God who is *for* the downtrodden, *for* the poor, *for* the oppressed, and *for* the least of society. Its dramatic culmination is an event unlike any other in history—we call it the Passion of the Christ. This, too, is a story from below, where a figure named Jesus offers a portrait of God unlike any other, where God is not a lion but a lamb. God is not a death dealer, but gives up his life in love for others. Thus, all who follow Jesus are to talk about God in light of the Cross, as that is where humanity and the divine most cohesively intersect.

So, what shall we do with the Bible then, given the various and often contradictory portraits of God it paints? Shall we break it up into dispensations, arguing that God changes as time goes by? Shall we just listen to Marcion and dismiss the entire Old Testament due to its portrayal of God as being violent? Or even more dramatic yet, shall we toss out the entire Bible—New Testament included—as post-enlightenment atheists strongly advise?

Ultimately, questions like these end up lacking in one regard or another. That has been my experience anyway. But, there is one whom I have found not to be lacking: *Jesus.* There is just something about him. And so, during our journey we will simply have to trust him to be our guide, our teacher, our master exegete. Hopefully then, we will discover just what that "something" about him actually is.

So let us journey together—and with Jesus—so that we can heal from our root causes of violence. Shalom, salaam, and in the words of our Lord Jesus Christ, "Peace be with you."

"Therefore also the Wisdom of God said, 'I will send them prophets and apostles, some of whom they will kill and persecute,' so that this generation may be charged with the blood of all the prophets shed since the foundation of the world, from the blood of Abel to the blood of Zechariah, who perished between the altar and the sanctuary. Yes, I tell you, it will be charged against this generation."

–LUKE 11:49-51

PART I

THE PROBLEM

CHAPTER 1

VIOLENCE: HUMANITY'S MOST PRESSING PROBLEM

"I object to violence because when it appears to do good, the good is only temporary; the evil it does is permanent."[1]

–MAHATMA GANDHI

At first glance, it may seem odd—perhaps heretical?—for a Christian author to begin a book with a quote by a Hindu, but I have been known to "bend the rules" over the past few years, so this should come as no surprise. Moreover, this is a book that primarily deals with the problem of violence, and then how to address it. So, I thought something from Gandhi would be fitting. It was, after all, Gandhi's firm—dare I say Christlike—stance on nonviolence that compelled a man named Nathuram Godse to fire three bullets into his chest. Peacefully standing up to the violent power structures is a sure way to suffer consequences. But Gandhi understood why he was called to follow Jesus' command, "If anyone strikes you on the right cheek, turn the other also" (Matt 5:39). He knew that returning violence with violence only perpetuates the problem, and the evil it causes always has lasting effects.

A heavily-influenced, and devoutly Christian, Martin Luther King Jr., also understood this.

As most of us well know, in spite of constant threats of violence, Dr. King never wavered in his commitment to peace. For thirteen years, he stood—or rather, marched—against the violent demon we call "racism," until it took his life in 1968. Like Gandhi, it was King's nonviolent way that led to violence against him. Since this has happened to so many others— Dietrich Bonhoeffer comes to mind—I cannot help but think that, perhaps, this is what Jesus meant when he said, "I have not come to bring peace, but a sword" (Matt 10:34). The powers and principalities do not take too kindly to those who would challenge their authority, yet some are called to challenge them nonetheless.

We, too, in our own way, will take up that challenge over the course of this journey.

That being said, let us take a step back and make sure we have a proper working definition for violence. I just posted something the other day on Facebook, reminding people how discussions and arguments should begin with definitions, so that dialogue is not thwarted on account of a misunderstanding. So I need to follow my own advice and do that here. The definition for violence that I will be working with in this book, then, comes from the World Health Organization, and reads: "the intentional use of physical force or power, threatened or actual, against oneself, another person, or against a group or community, which either results in or has the high likelihood of resulting in injury, death, psychological harm, maldevelopment, or deprivation."[2] The thing I would like to point out is that there is intent to do harm attached to this definition. And that is why I chose it, as

I believe that is the difference between some forms of force and actual violence. For example, I would not call it violent to push my five-year old daughter out of the way of a moving car. Sure, she may fall down and bang her knee on the sidewalk, but the intent is to do well by her, namely, to save her from being hit by the car. I hope you see the difference, then, between some force and violence.

So, with this as our working understanding, throughout this chapter we will take a bird's eye look at a wide range of evidence—both statistical and experiential—that shows just how harmful and destructive human violence has been and continues to be. And while most of us are aware of this fact, we take this survey in order to really get a better—or should I say, bitter—taste of our plight.

Disclaimer: *This chapter is not for the faint of heart!*

WAR, WHAT IS IT GOOD FOR? ABSOLUTELY NOTHING!

Throughout history, war has been the inhumane means through which groups of people—whether tribes, nations, empires, or religious sects—have secured self-interest by using extreme violence against other groups, even to the point of genocide. Humanity has engaged in war primarily over land disputes, resource allocation, and of course, the "wills of the gods." This is not even to mention the litany of other reasons too numerous to list. The human cost has been astronomical, and, sadly, we are still paying the price today. Below are the estimated death tolls for the top ten bloodiest wars in human history:[3]

1. Mongol Conquests (1206–1324): 40–70 million

2. World War II (1939–1945): 40–60 million

3. Three Kingdoms/End of the Han Dynasty (184–280): 36–40 million

4. Second Sino-Japanese War (1937–1945): 25 million

5. Qing Dynasty conquest of the Ming Dynasty (1616–1662): 25 million

6. Taiping Rebellion (1850–1864): 20–100 million

7. World War I (1914–1918): 20 million

8. An Lushan Rebellion (755–763): 13–36 million

9. Dungan Revolt (1862–1877): 8–20 million

10. Chinese Civil War (1927–1949): 8 million

I should point out that these figures include civilians who were not involved directly in the fight but who were targets and/ or victims nonetheless. This list even includes direct and premeditated attacks on civilians throughout the more "enlightened" twentieth and twenty-first centuries. For instance, on August 6 and August 8, 1945, the United States dropped two atomic bombs on the cities of Hiroshima and Nagasaki, Japan. The combined death toll of both events, although impossible to estimate precisely due to the overwhelming chaos created, was in the hundreds of thousands. More recently, on September 11, 2001, two airplanes crashed into the World Trade Center in New York, knocking down *three* buildings and killing nearly 3,000 civilians. The most recent major crisis is the Syrian Civil War, which has led to the death of an estimated 220,000 people (as of January 15, 2015).[4] It has also displaced millions more, with Syrian refugees continuing to flee (and perish) as I write this book. Ironically, but not surprisingly, this is all taking place *nearly* one hundred years after the end of the "war to end all wars."[5] Although I hope he is wrong, I cannot help but think how prophetic Albert Einstein now sounds, "I know not with what weapons World War III will be fought, but World War IV will be fought with sticks and stones."[6]

A FIRST-HAND LOOK AT THE MISERY OF WAR

"They wrote in the old days that it is sweet and fitting to die for one's country. But in modern war there is nothing sweet nor fitting in your dying. You will die like a dog for no good reason."[7]

—ERNEST HEMINGWAY

Because the truth of war is not explained with statistics, but rather, through firsthand experience, I want to allow a few of those who have actually experienced the horrors of war do most of the talking in this section. They are the ones throughout the course of history who have witnessed real human beings bleeding real human blood. They are the ones who have witnessed children and adults alike being massacred in extraordinary numbers. The truth of war, then, comes from their stories.

Since I already mentioned the devastation that befell Hiroshima, Japan, I would like to begin there. The following is Ms. Akiko Takakura's account of the horror she discovered in her city the day the bomb fell:

> Many people on the street were killed almost instantly. The fingertips of those dead bodies caught fire and the fire gradually spread over their entire bodies from their fingers. A light gray liquid dripped down their hands, scorching their fingers. I, I was so shocked to know that fingers and bodies could be burned and deformed like that. I just couldn't believe it. It was horrible. And looking at it, it was more painful for me to think how the

fingers were burned, hands and fingers that would hold babies or turn pages, they just, they just burned away.[8]

Sadly, this sort of scene was expected by those like theoretical physicist J. Robert Oppenheimer, who worked to develop the atomic bomb under the infamous moniker "The Manhattan Project." His quote from the 1965 documentary, *The Decision to Drop the Bomb*, remains one of the most chilling things ever said.

> We knew the world would not be the same. A few people laughed, a few people cried, most people were silent. I remembered the line from the Hindu scripture, the Bhagavad-Gita; Vishnu is trying to persuade the Prince that he should do his duty and, to impress him, takes on his multi-armed form and says, "Now I am become Death, the destroyer of worlds." I suppose we all thought that, one way or another.[9]

Atomic weapons gave humanity the ability to become a new type of death-dealer, one so great that we would begin to define ourselves as synonymous with death itself.

For another eyewitness account from World War II, we now head over to the European Theatre, to hear from Mordechai Ronen, a survivor of the Shoah.[10] He explains the conditions of multiple Nazi concentration camps, including the dreaded Auschwitz.

> They gave us food in barrels. When the barrel was empty, I could get inside and scrape the leftovers from the bottom. In that way my dad and I got extra food. I remember the chimneys were dark, thick smoke rising from them; dogs barking all the time. From Auschwitz, they moved us to Birkenau, then to Mauthasen-Gusen. Every morning there were dead bodies along the barbed wire fences around the camp. The electrified fences instantly killed anyone who touched them. Perhaps these were simply acts of suicide. When we were in Gusen penal camp, my father, who was fifty, one day just gave up and said he couldn't continue. From that moment I was totally alone. In February

1945 they moved us to Gunskirchen, Upper Austria. It was here that I witnessed starving people eating human flesh.[11]

Ronen's testimony, while heartbreaking and difficult to read, is sadly not all that unique. The sheer numbers of Jews, Poles, Soviets, gypsies, and others who entered these death camps is astounding. What is equally as shocking is the number of those who perished. Although the totals will never be known, what we do know is that there were over 850 of those camps and, within the walls and fences of some of the most brutal, upwards of 900,000 lives were lost.[12]

Next, we travel to nineteenth-century United States of America, who in the war for territory and, quite arrogantly, for "destiny," performed heinous acts of terror against those who had made this land their home millennia prior. Elizabeth Watts, a Cherokee woman, heartbreakingly explains the horror discovered along the "Trail of Tears:"

> The soldiers gathered them up, all up, and put them in camps. They hunted them and ran them down until they got all of them. Even before they were loaded in wagons, many of them got sick and died. They were all grief stricken they lost all on earth they had. White men even robbed their dead's graves to get their jewelry and other little trinkets. They saw to stay was impossible and Cherokees told General Scott they would go without further trouble and the long journey started. They did not all come at once. First one batch and then another. The sick, old, and babies rode on the grub and household wagons. The best rode a horse, if they had one. Most of them walked. Many of them died along the way. They buried them where they died, in unmarked graves. The road they traveled, history calls the "Trail of Tears." This trail was more than tears. It was death, sorrow, hunger, exposure, and humiliation to a civilized people as were the Cherokees.[13]

To put this in a bit of perspective, what we are talking about with the "Trail of Tears" is the removal of roughly 16,000

Cherokee from their native land, 4,000 of which died during the three year forced migration.[14] What we are talking about is less than 200 years ago, and done by a nation founded on "Judeo-Christian principles," as I am often reminded. I say that not to be anti-American or anti-Christian, but rather, to point out that not even *my* country or *my religion* is immune to violence.

Stories like these, from just a few of humanity's more infamous conflicts, were unfortunately not terribly difficult to find, and sadly, are only the tip of the iceberg. I could have included accounts from the Rwandan Genocide, the "killing fields" of Cambodia under the Khmer Rouge, Stalin's Gulags, the Spanish Inquisition, the Great Chinese Famine under Mao Zedong, and so many more. The point is that it is easy to see why humankind can identify itself with death, as Oppenheimer hauntingly observed. All we have to do is look at the evidence and listen to the voices on the other end of whatever weapon we happen to be wielding at the time.

Now, before we move on to discuss the secondary crises that arise due to war, I would like to conclude with one final first-hand account of its horrors. In a way, this one will hit a little closer to home, as I will turn to my good friend, Staff Sergeant Dominic Moes, who is now medically retired after having spent ten years serving as a soldier in the United States Army. Concerning the current crisis in the Middle East, he writes:

> Upon joining the US Army—to serve my country as a Military Police—I, like everyone else, signed on the dotted line, that I was "willing to defend the US Constitution unto death." Of course, this death was preferably the death of my enemies and if need be even "death by nuke" to those deemed "enemy" of the United States. I slapped my signature down without a second thought—after all, *we have to do what we have to do in order to protect the sanctity of our sovereign nation.* At least those were my thoughts at the time.

During my 2006/2007 deployment—in support of Operation Iraqi Freedom—I was an M2 gunner (.50 caliber machine gun). Every day, I racked rounds into my M2 and made the decision that anyone who dared engage our squad was going to get mowed down by my hand. That might sound morbid to some, but it would be less painful and quicker than the "bayonet-inflicted-death" we ritualistically "chanted" about during basic training. In the mind of a soldier, nothing is more glorious.

Drill Sergeant: "What makes the green grass grow?"

Trainee: "Blood, blood, bright red blood, Drill Sergeant!"

Day by day, mission upon mission, things never changed. They only got worse. Death became a new reality for us. And so, after a while, we just stopped caring about life because it could end at any moment.

After coming home from my "glorious" tour of war, I soon realized that everything I believed prior to joining the Army was false. I had bought into the lie that there was glory in war. After experiencing the killing, the death, and fear and hate and rage that accompanies the atrocities of war, the truth became plain as day; there is no glory in war.[15]

THE SECONDARY PROBLEMS OF COMBAT

In this section, we will be discussing two secondary crises that arise because of war and conflict, namely food shortages and ecological disasters. Certainly, there are more than just two, but these are the most obvious as well as the most devastating.

Food Shortages

The link between war and famine has long been noted. Anthropologist Ellen Messer offers a broad explanation as to how this correlation works.

> Food shortage ripples into the larger economy and extends over multiple years when farmers, herders, and others flee attacks,

terror, and destruction or suffer reductions in their capacities to produce food because of forced labor recruitment (including conscription) and war-related depletion of assets. Ancillary attacks of disease, linked to destruction of health facilities, and hardship and hunger also reduce the human capacity for food production. These factors set the stage for multiple years of food shortage.[16]

We have witnessed this reduction of the "human capacity for food production" that Messer mentions, most notably, in the destruction of the rice paddies during the Vietnam War.[17] These were actions that of course were defended and "justified," as they were deemed necessary to cut off food supply to the enemy, but in reality they were premeditated acts of eco-terrorism against civilians nonetheless—and the human cost was great.[18] Dr. Ngo Vinh Long, professor of history at the University of Maine, explains just how great the devastation was:

> The Thieu regime…felt confident enough to carry out an "economic blockade" designed to inflict hunger and starvation on the PRG [*Provisional Revolutionary Government*] areas. Thieu was frequently quoted as exhorting his armed forces to do their utmost to implement the "economic blockade" in order to defeat the "Communists" by starving them out. This blockade, which was also known as the "rice war" in the American press at the time, included prohibitions on the transport of rice from one village to another, rice-milling by anyone except the government, storage of rice in homes, and the sale of rice outside the village to any except government-authorized buyers. Widespread hunger and starvation were the results. According to reports by Saigon deputies and Catholic priests, up to 60 percent of the population of the central provinces were reduced to eating bark, cacti, banana roots, and the bulbs of wild grass. Children and the aged were the first victims. In some central Vietnam villages, deaths from starvation reached 1 to 2 percent of the total population each month.[19]

Bahr el-Ghazal in South Sudan offers us another instance where we witness a strong correlation between war and famine. Here, in 1988, roughly 250,000 Sudanese civilians died due to the civil war and the subsequent food shortage that ensued.[20] Ten years later, in nearly cyclical fashion, that country experienced another 70,000 fatalities for very similar reasons.[21]

Similar consequences arise when even more "non-violent" approaches to combat, such as economic sanctions, are placed on countries. For example, during the first five years after sanctions were placed on Iraq in 1993, an estimated 500,000 Iraqi children died due to rising food and health care costs.[22] While sanctions were placed on the government, it was the "lower-class" citizens, often children, who experienced direct repercussions. And, like the sanctions placed on the Vietnamese, they were even labeled "worth it" by former Secretary of State Madeleine Albright.[23] No matter the country, no matter the conflict, the end result is almost always the same.

Ecological Disasters

Although it is impossible to count the exact ecological costs of war, they are immense nonetheless. According to some experts, they are so great that the survival of our species is at risk. Public health researcher Dr. Jennifer Leaning warns:

> The escalating numbers of weapons and the diverse technologies of destruction and delivery now available to virtually any country that wishes to pay the price, place the local, regional, and global environments in greater jeopardy than ever before. Chemical and biological weapons, cluster bombs, fuel-air explosives, and herbicides are capable of inflicting massive and lasting damage on natural ecosystems and thus threatening [sic] the survival of entire human populations. Any war between forces equipped with these modern systems carries the potential of creating as much environmental destruction as the Gulf War.[24]

In case you may not be aware of the vast ecological disaster that was created due to the Gulf War, not only was the fragile desert ecosystem impacted by the constant bombardment of weaponry, but so too was the region's drinking water, especially in Saudi Arabia and Kuwait.[25] This was due in large part to the sabotaging of hundreds of oil wells and lakes in the area by the Iraqi military after coalition forces advancements. The long-term effects in the region have been astronomical and if something like this were to happen on a global scale, it could have untold implications.

Human technology is wonderful, but it is also dangerous. Across the globe, we can bear witness to the devastation that we are capable of, even when there is not violence involved. From the disaster caused by Fukushima in 2011 and at Chernobyl roughly a quarter-century prior, to the fallout after the aforementioned Hiroshima and Nagasaki bombings, our technological advances have also led to the cause of some of our greatest ecological disasters. Should we fail to learn from this, we run the risk of an extinction of our species, as Dr. Leaning cautions against.

VIOLENCE IN SUBTLER FORMS

The subtler but still destructive form of violence is that of *structural violence*, a term introduced by Norwegian sociologist Johan Galtung. Whereas direct violence is more obvious and overt, structural violence is, at least on the surface, more restrained. It is witnessed whenever one group of people is assumed to have more opportunities, whether economically or socially, than another group. As peace advocate Rajkumar Bobichand discerns: "This unequal advantage is built into the very social, political and economic systems that govern societies, states, and the world."[26] Let's explore a few examples.

JIM CROW LAWS

Jim Crow laws were laws that enforced racial segregation in the southern United States up until 1965. What resulted from this "cultural norm" was that black public facilities were constantly second-rate when compared to their white counterparts. Sociologist David Pilgrim describes it as follows:

> There were separate hospitals for blacks and whites, separate prisons, separate public and private schools, separate churches, separate cemeteries, separate public restrooms, and separate public accommodations. In most instances, the black facilities were grossly inferior—generally, older, less-well-kept. In other cases, there were no black facilities—no Colored public restroom, no public beach, no place to sit or eat.[27]

While these laws did in fact lead to direct violence, such as lynching, they were also *structurally* violent as they provided whites with more opportunities than blacks, ensuring that the status-quo which kept blacks in subservience to whites remained ever-present.

THE WAR ON DRUGS

Another set of laws that are structurally violent against blacks are those that make up the United States' War on Drugs. Did you know that of the roughly 225,000 people incarcerated in 2011 for state drug offenses, 45 percent were black, while just 30 percent were white?[28] This, is in spite of the fact that, as Huffington Post's Saki Knafo reports, "White Americans are more likely than black Americans to have used most kinds of illegal drugs, including cocaine, marijuana and LSD."[29] John McWhorter, associate professor of linguistics at the University of California, Berkeley, paints the following picture in an attempt to enlighten others about the truth of this supposed War on Drugs.

Let's imagine a black America with no War on Drugs. No more gang wars over turf, no more kids shooting each other over sneakers, no more "Stop the Violence" rallies, no more agonized discussions about gun possession in the inner city. Quite simply, people who don't sell drugs for a living don't much need to kill each other over turf…If we truly want to get past race in this country, we must be aware that it will never happen until the futile War on Drugs so familiar to us now is a memory. All it will take is a single generation of black Americans growing up in a post-Prohibition America for us to get where we all want to go. The time to end the War on Drugs, therefore, is yesterday.[30]

While I may not agree with the universality of some of McWhorter's statements, what I do agree with is the fact that ending the War on Drugs would not only *lower* the rate of violence that is directly correlated with the prohibition of any substance, but it would also end the structural violence it perpetuates against blacks. It may not eradicate "kids shooting each other over sneakers," but it will certainly spring humanity forward toward a more peaceful world.

MARRIAGE INEQUALITY

Marriage equality has been a hot button topic for quite some time—and for good reason. Prior to 2015, the United States federal government did not recognize LGBT marriage (although some states did). Unless you have been under a rock for the past few years, you know everything has since changed, which is a good thing, because I believe the federal government's previous stance on marriage was *the* classic case of structural violence: declaring that one group of people should be afforded something another group is not. That is to say, whereas the straight person could choose to wed a romantic partner from within the group whom he/she is already predisposed to, the LGBT person could not. Or, in other words, the straight person could be married to the one whom they *love* and be afforded all the benefits and rights that come with that union, while the LGBT person could not. Sure, they could share a residence together and call themselves a "union," but they could not be declared "married." And sure, it may be subtler than the carpet bombing of a city, but it is violent nonetheless—*structurally*—which based on the recent shootings in Orlando can even turn *directly* violent. Sadly, this is not unique. Take the following from a 1999 *Washington Post* article entitled "Police Link Brothers to Christian Identity."

> The Williams brothers, who are being held without bail, each have been charged with murder, robbery and burglary. The indictment alleges that earlier this month the two men killed a prominent gay couple in Redding, Gary Matson and Winfield Scott Mowder, because of their "sexual orientation." (...) Both brothers, who were raised in a fundamentalist Christian family in California, were armed with semiautomatic weapons and one was wearing a bulletproof vest when they were apprehended, police said.[31]

When a culture embraces an "us vs. them" mentality the structural violence engrained within the society has the potential for direct violence against "them." Additionally, it has the potential to create psychological terror for those the violence is directed at, as we too often witness. For one such example, I want to introduce you to my good friend, Robert Lofgren, who has had the misfortune of having been terrorized by this culture-structuring violence. What he will have to say requires great vulnerability, but he does so bravely anyway.

> From the moment I was a baby, I was in church every time the doors were open. Like most good Evangelicals, we were not only taught about God's love and grace, but also that God was a God of holiness and wrath. In a plainly dualistic way, it

seemed we could not talk about God's love without also talking about his wrath.

From a very young age, I sensed that there was something different about me—I did not feel like I quite fit in with the other boys. It was when I hit puberty when I knew that there was something horribly different about me—something utterly sinful, something to be ashamed about, something that would cause a great amount of anxiety and trauma in my life. This something was that I was gay.

But I was not supposed to "claim that as my identity." At least, that was what I was told. To refer to myself as gay was to align myself with my sin nature—to be rebellious toward Jesus Christ. I learned as a young pre-teen that I was an abomination before God—and thus would experience his wrath—but also that there was somehow the hope of salvation

Placed before me were two options. First, I could get Christian counseling and pray that perhaps God would give me natural desires for women. There were others who were *supposedly* successful—the Evangelical Church lifted them up as shining examples that change and healing were possible. The second option was a lifetime of celibacy. After all, this was my "thorn in the flesh," and maybe God would never remove it from me. Maybe this "struggle" was predestined for me as a way to draw near to God.

If I did not follow these two options set before me, then I was told that I was essentially shaking my fist at God, that I was following the broad road that leads to destruction, and living a "lifestyle" that would certainly lead me to the eternal flames of hell.

These teachings, which I believed because I heard them taught over and over again riddled my whole being with fear, anxiety, depression, and disillusion. I could never see myself loving a woman as a heterosexual man could, even though I believed that God was capable of the miraculous. After all, I had been praying for years, I read some books by various ex-gay authors, and even received some counseling throughout Bible College, yet I never received any healing. If my only other option was celibacy, I thought that perhaps I could succeed. Maybe with God's help and with the help of my church community, I could stick it out. But as the years went on and I saw my friends married off, one-by-one, I got lonelier and lonelier. As I grew older, I started wondering what would become of me. I started to wonder who would be there if I were ever struck down with illness—who would hold my hand, sing to me, whisper they love me, and kiss my face as I lay dying?

Jesus said that his yoke was easy and that his burdens were light, and if we believed and followed him that we would find an abundant life, that rivers of living water would flow from within us, and that we would never thirst again. So why couldn't this be true for me, why didn't it seem to be true for any LGBTQ people within the conservative Church? If I truly was following sound doctrine, why wasn't I—why weren't we—producing good fruit? Why were we depressed, addicted, and suicidal?

Evangelicalism brought me to a place of despair. As a way to self-medicate, and to temporarily forget my problems, I turned to alcohol. And when I formed a long-term relationship with another man, sadly, I brought these struggles into the partnership. And even though I have since discovered healing, and have found an affirming community and a new way to understand the Scriptures—as well as a healthier view of human sexuality—I can still feel the lasting effects of my experiences with Evangelicalism. I can still feel the scars, and am still a bit haunted.[32]

VIOLENCE AS A CULTURAL NORM

If we turn out attention back to the subject of direct violence, we will notice in some cultures, such as that of the United States, violence becomes so central to how the norms of society are defined, that it transcends nearly every aspect of it. Perhaps this is but one symptom of a country that has more or less been at war since its inception, as the United States most emphatically has.

Take a stroll through the aisles at your favorite toy store and notice the inundation of weapons and wartime memorabilia. Head to your local movie theater and chances are you will end up seeing three different commercials for different US Military branches before the film starts (as I recently did). In fact, the motion picture industry is so obsessed with violence that of the top ten grossing films of 2015, seven featured violence front and center throughout (*The Hunger Games: Mockingjay Part II, Star Wars: The Force Awakens, Mission: Impossible—Rogue Nation, Spectre, Avengers: Age of Ultron, Furious 7,* and *Jurassic World*).[33] But, to be fair, the motion picture industry is just giving us what we desire.

And sadly, so too are our clergy.

On November 11, 2015, two days after the terrorist attacks that killed 130 people in Paris, France, Robert Jeffress, pastor of First Baptist Church, had this to say to his congregation:

> God has empowered the government, the military, to bring wrath against those who practice evil. You may not agree with everything Donald Trump says but Donald Trump was absolutely correct Thursday night when he said, "It is time to start bombing the 'you-know-what' out of ISIS." That is a biblical response.[34]

Or, take Jerry Falwell Jr., President of Liberty University, who said this to his students after the terrorist attacks in San Bernardino, California:

> If some of those people in that community center had what I've got in my back pocket right now…is it illegal to pull it out? I don't know. I've always thought if more good people had concealed-carry permits, then we could end those Muslims before they walked in…and killed them [sic].[35]

In each instance, less than a half-week after a major violent attack, two of America's "Christian faith leaders" took to the microphone to boldly proclaim that violence should be used to thwart violence. Now, I will not delve into what the appropriate response should be to radicalized terrorism (as addressing the context for why entities like ISIS exist in the first place would be a book in itself), but what I will simply suggest is that a *posture* where violence is so wholeheartedly embraced as the only means with which to solve the world's toughest problems is a tell-tale sign of a culture *obsessed* with such a method. I believe we live in just such a culture, as we find strong evidence of this, not only in our retail stores and movie theaters, but also on our televisions, in our universities, and sadly, in our churches on Sundays.

SOME FINAL THOUGHTS

Pre-Socratic Greek philosopher Heraclitus argued that the *logos*, that is, the "structuring principle of reality," of human civilization is violence and (as we have discussed over the course of this chapter) "war is the father of all and king of all."[36] That is to say, according to Heraclitus, our human cultures are held together and maintained by violence. To show how Heraclitus' assessment is apt, first, we have explored the evidence of the devastation from the most obvious manifestation of violence—the "father" and "king" of all—that of war. Moreover, we have noticed how violence is not merely encapsulated in direct forms, but also in indirect forms, in structural forms, some of which cyclically lead back to direct forms of violence. Sadly, violence has the potential to become so commonplace that social norms are centered on and perpetuated by it.

That being said, over the course of the next two chapters, we will turn our attention to the work of two great thinkers, René Girard and Ernest Becker, as each offer compelling insight into what the root causes of humanity's violence are. From there, we will search for some solutions, which, although probably surprising to some, will be found in the very same Scriptures many, such as Robert Jeffress and Jerry Falwell Jr., use to *justify* violence in the first place.

CHAPTER 2

ROOT CAUSE #1: MIMETIC DESIRE

"Desire can be the most life-giving force, inspiring us to give our-selves completely to another; it can also be a most destructive force, causing us to harm others and ourselves." [1]

–ANDRÉ RABE

O ver the course of this chapter, we will be exploring what I am calling the first root cause of violence, namely that of *mimetic desire*.[2] Most of what any have to say about this concept comes from the work of late French anthropologist René Girard. It is he who is to thank for developing the mimetic theory, which I will also be fleshing out the details of throughout the chapter and then also later in this book, when I begin to discuss the Scriptures. I will contend that it is this theory that really explains who we are as a species, and just as when Darwin, reflecting upon his own theory of the species, penned, "much light will be thrown on the origin of man and his history,"[3] so too more light has been thrown due to the work of Girard.

RENÉ GIRARD

A BRIEF BACKGROUND

René Girard was born in Avignon, France on December 25, 1923.[4] In 1947, after studying at *l'École des Chartes* in France—writing his dissertation on fifteenth-century Avignon marriage and private life—he moved to the United States and began attending Indiana University, earning his PhD three years later in 1950.[5] Although he primarily studied history, the university commissioned him to teach French, where he had his students read some of the French greats like Proust, Flaubert, and Stendhal (I will explain why this is important in the following section). In addition to Indiana University, Girard also taught at Bryn Mawr College, Duke University, Johns Hopkins University, and then most notably, at Stanford University, from 1981 until 1995.

Over the course of his entire career, in addition to teaching, Girard published an abundance of works, including dozens of acclaimed books. Throughout our discussion, we will primarily be drawing from three, namely *Violence and the Sacred*, *Things Hidden since the Foundation of the World*, and *I See Satan Fall like Lightning*.

FROM LITERATURE TO ANTHROPOLOGY

While Girard was teaching French, he noticed that the characters in the literary works of the great writers—like Dostoyevsky and Shakespeare, in addition to the likes of Proust, Flaubert, and Stendhal—displayed certain behaviors that up until that point had no concrete explanation. He picked up on the fact that the desires of the characters were based on the desires of other characters and vice versa. That is to say, *mimesis* (Greek for "imitation") was the driving force for the characters' desires. To put it in the simplest of terms, they were all essentially copycats of each other. In Girard's first book, *Deceit, Desire, and the Novel* (1959), he lays out this profound idea for the first time.

From literature, Girard moved into the world of anthropology and sure enough, noticed that this mimetic desire is not merely confined to the characters created from within the minds of the world's greatest writers, but rather, that it is foundational to the characters of the real life human drama we all take part in. The truth, Girard discovered, is that all of us desire not only what material items and personal qualities each other possess, but that we also desire the very desires of the other.

So, how does this work?

Well, to answer that question, we will first turn to the field of psychology and travel all the way back to the moment of our birth. There, we will discover something quite vital to how we understand the human being, which in turn, will allow us to then be able to unravel these uniquely human complexities.

LEARNING THROUGH IMITATION

Contrary to what developmental psychologist Jean Piaget argued, which is that we learn *how* to imitate each other after birth, humans actually learn, from birth, *by* imitating. (We have psychologists Andrew Meltzoff and Keith Moore to thank for first solidifying an understanding of this phenomenon.) Psychologist Jean-Michel Oughourlian explains that imitation is what makes learning possible in the first place and that "through imitation and repetition the child gradually acquires his parents' language and little by little their entire culture."[6] So too will the child begin to desire what "mommy and daddy" desire simply because they desire it. Because of this imitation, where the notion of the self is derived by the other, Girard coined the term "interdividual."[7]

As a father, I have no doubt noticed this sort of non-conscious imitation.[8] Just as Oughourlian contends, little by little, my five year old daughter has imitated "mommy and daddy" so much so that she hardly sticks out in our twenty-first century American culture. She, at age five now, speaks the English language proficiently, can tell you all about each Disney princess, and bears the influence of some very skilled ballet instructors. Her imitation of those around her is quite clear.

Now, this sort of imitation is not seen only in children though. As adults—yes, even "autonomous" Americans—we learn and desire because of imitation. There are literally thousands of examples we could turn to in order to display this: from modeling for new mechanics how to properly change a spark plug, to physicians who model how to perform the most complex of brain surgeries to younger surgeons, and everything in between. My favorite though is when a guy on a putt-putt golfing date wraps his arms around his girlfriend and shows her how to grip the putter. (I must admit that I have done this myself.) Throughout our entire lives, we never stop learning, nor desiring, through the process of imitation.

I DESIRE, YOU DESIRE, WE DESIRE

Alright, what is so bad about desiring what the other desires? Well, before we answer that directly, I will say that it is not necessarily bad per se, but rather, human. And because it is a foundational part of what makes us "human," I would agree with Girard when he says that it is actually "intrinsically good."[9] Girard explains what separates us from the rest of the animal kingdom: "Humankind is a creature who lost a part of its animal instinct in order to gain access to 'desire,' as it is called. Once their natural needs are satisfied, humans desire intensely, but they don't know exactly what they desire, for no instinct guides them."[10] Should a human being's desire indeed be fixed, they would be no different than other species. Surely, what constitutes "human" would be lost. Allow me to include a graphic to help explain:

PERSON A   PERSON B   11

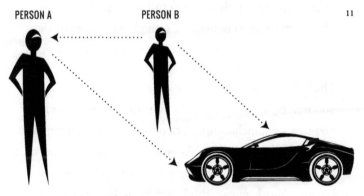

PERSON B NOTICES PERSON A'S DESIRE FOR THE
SPORTS CAR. PERSON B THEN DESIRES THE CAR.

That being said, even though mimetic desire is not a bad thing, there is a cautionary element to it, which I will now address.

My friends and colleagues at *The Raven ReView* have a great poster on their website, explaining three common, everyday problems that arise because of humanity's mimetic desire. I will be turning to these in order to elucidate what Girard describes as "scandal," which translates to "stumbling block" in both Hebrew and Greek,[12] and comes to pass because of our inability to grasp that which we desire. Here are the three scenarios in their entirety.

The Playroom
Imagine a small child in a room full of toys. He is only casually engaged with a toy nearby. Another child enters

the room and surveys the toys. Which one will she choose? It will most likely be the toy the first child seems interested in, because even that casual interest makes that toy more desirable than all the others. As she reaches for the toy, the first child's interest is suddenly enflamed. He may shout, "I had it first!" and tussle with her for possession of an object he hardly desired until she seemed to want it. They may come to blows over something neither of them wanted all that badly until the other wanted it, too.

The Sale Table

You pass by a sale table with a number of things you have no interest in, including a stack of blue sweaters much like the one you are wearing. As you linger nearby, someone stops and picks up one of the sweaters, which piques your interest. You begin to think that your blue sweater is a bit shabby and that the one he's holding seems so much better than yours. In fact, it now seems much better than the others on the table. You instinctively realize that if you were to show interest in the sweaters, the other shopper might realize what a great bargain he has in his hands and hang on to it. So you feign disinterest so as not to fuel his desire. Your tactic works, he drops the sweater and leaves.

Love Triangles

Why do two friends often fall in love with the same person? Because friends are used to sharing and enflaming each other's desires. Friends enjoy introducing each other to new things and "falling in love" with them together. Whether it's a book, movie, entertainer or fashion designer, if one friend has a lukewarm reaction, the other friend's interest will wane, too. So when it comes to lovers, if Jake is head over heels in love, it's very natural for his friend Bob to feel the same way. Often Jake might actually want Bob to be a bit gaga for his significant other because he is used to having his desires reinforced and encouraged by Bob. Unfortunately, both friends are usually ignorant of this dynamic. If Bob believes his love is "true" and authentic, the friendship may turn to rivalry. Or if Bob feels so-so, Jake's love may quickly fade.[13]

As you can see, these types of rivalries that we witness are a day-to-day occurrence. They are enflamed and then most often dealt with in the moment (save for the third example perhaps). However, when the rivalry cannot be solved in the moment—if the violence has to be deferred—then energy and hostility builds up and grows like a cancer of sorts.[14] Hatred may grow within the person and they may use this as motivation to enact vengeance on the other.[15] In fact, this violent retribution is often more than "an eye for an eye" as the saying goes, but rather, an eye for an eye plus something more. Regarding retribution, Michael Hardin, drawing from studies done at the University of Texas, writes: "the aggressor thinks they are giving exactly what was given but the person who is being hit knows there has been an escalation, however slight, and so another greater blow must be given in order to level the playing field."[16]

This escalating desire to have our wrath propitiated can be observed on a larger scale than the day-to-day examples I just used. The first one that comes to mind can be witnessed in places like the streets of America's urban centers. It is found in gang violence, or in what is known as turf wars. I bore witness to this during my twenties, when I worked at the local juvenile hall and then in a handful of youth group homes, with some of California's toughest young gang members. Hypothetical stories like the following would be all too commonplace:

A Norteño walks down the street, but on the wrong side, the Sureño side in fact. Because of this, five Sureños run up on the kid and beat him to within an inch of his life. Then they hurry off before they get caught. But when the young Norteño's fellow gang members find him, they know who is responsible. So they plot something big, something that would "send those scraps a message."[17] They wait until a few Sureños are out on the street, alone. Then twenty or so Norteños come out of nowhere, with knives and brass knuckles, and brutally beat all five of the Sureños, killing two of them and sending one other to the ICU. Now, there is only *one thing* for the Sureños to do…

As dissimilar as the warring gangs believed themselves to be, it was actually their *similarities* that stood out. All of their retribution and escalating hostility toward one another was a reflection of the other. Their colors may have been different—Norteño red and Sureño blue—but their actions were a classic case of mimetic rivalry. Surely, the turf each desired was fed by the others' desire for it, but as we have discussed, both could not possibly possess it.

Now, if the above example was not two California gangs but rather, an entire community or civilization, this mimetic rivalry would have the potential to destroy everyone. That is because, unlike other species in the animal kingdom, who generally submit to the dominant member of the pack when defeat is recognized, human beings escalate violence to the point of killing each other over something, even when the initial conflict is often not even recognized or recalled (like in the above example).

THE TRANSFERENCE OF VIOLENCE

What Girard noticed takes place while a community is spiraling out of control, when the violence of *all against all* is so great that the civilization may collapse, is that the transference of violence occurs. It is displaced onto one member (or subgroup) of the community and in doing so, *unites* the community, creating cohesion where there was none before. This phenomenon is called the *scapegoating mechanism*. Girard explains: "Where only shortly before a thousand individual conflicts had raged unchecked between a thousand enemy brothers, there now reappears a true community, united in its hatred for one alone of its number. All the rancors scattered at random among the divergent individuals, all the differing antagonisms, now converge on an isolated and unique figure, the surrogate victim."[18] The following figure offers a visualization of this.

[19]

And you know what? This process works! When violence is transferred from *all against all* to *all against one*, peace does in fact ensue. However, it is always temporary, as the process inevitably repeats itself as the community progresses through history; every time new rivalries arise.[20]

And who plays the role of the scapegoat?

Generally, it is a person or group of persons who stand out from the rest of the community; people with deformities, psychological issues, and odd personality traits, for instance. The scapegoat is often minority cultural and racial groups, those with "alternative" sexual dispositions, and, because of our political nature, kings, presidents, and prime ministers.[21] To help us understand this better, I would like to journey back to some of the cultures we explored in chapter 1, as well as introduce one other, showing how their victimage is the product of scapegoating.

JAPANESE-AMERICANS IN THE UNITED STATES IN THE 1940S

On December 7, 1941, the United States of America was attacked at Pearl Harbor by the Japanese Empire (led by Hideki Tojo). One day later, the United States declared war. Shortly thereafter, President Franklin D. Roosevelt signed Executive Order 9066, which then led to the imprisonment of roughly 120,000 Japanese Americans.[22] The rationale behind suspending the writ of *habeas corpus*[23] for citizens of Japanese descent was that they were deemed "a threat to national security," something many in the United States agreed with, as an anti-Japanese posture was already established prior to the beginning of World War II.[24]

If only we could rid ourselves of the Japanese, then the United States of America could have peace!

After the "date which will live in infamy," *that* attitude intensified. "Japs," as they were derogatorily called, were often depicted as monkeys and gorillas in the media.[25] Propaganda films, such as *Japanese Relocation* (1943) and *A Challenge to Democracy* (1944), inaccurately portrayed the incarcerated Japanese-Americans as being pleased to be in the camps, rather than devastated to be uprooted in such an inhumane way, as was the reality of their plight. Newspapers up and down the West Coast spoke positively about the camps, deeming them necessary and vital for the safety of the nation. This, of course, was all a fabrication in order to gain the support of the American people, to unite against a common enemy. After all, for the scapegoating mechanism to work, all fingers need to be pointing the accusatory finger in the same direction. In this case, for a handful of harsh years at least, that finger pointed directly at Japanese-Americans.

JEWS IN NAZI GERMANY DURING THE 1940S

In similar, albeit vastly more brutal fashion was the Nazi scapegoating of the Jews. As we explored in chapter 1, the concentration camps Jews and other "undesirables" were forced into were most inhumane. In order to justify treating human beings in this manner, Jews had to be portrayed in an extremely negative fashion. They had to be defined as the enemy of the "chosen people," the Aryans. Harvard University's Karthik Narayanaswami explains how this happened:

> Jews were either portrayed as seedy, degenerate, ugly, masses associated with vermin, or they were portrayed as greedy, fat, and unpleasant elements who sided with the enemy. There is a reason why the Nazis chose such a portrayal, and why this even worked in the first place…To elicit the Bandwagon Effect in an "Us vs. Them" portrayal of an unpleasant looking Jewish caricature…The "Us vs. Them" theme became particularly explicit as Germany began its war on aggression, and showed a picture-perfect German mother and child, contrasted with an abject

poverty-stricken Bolshevik family, with a man who resembles the Nazi Jewish caricatures."[26]

According to the Nazis, Hitler's perfect world could never be a reality if the Jews were around.

If only we could rid ourselves of the Jews, then Nazi Germany could be made great again!

Because of this sort of mentality, as we all know, the Jewish people, as well as other "undesirables," were then slaughtered by the millions.

THE LGBT COMMUNITY DURING THE TWENTY-FIRST CENTURY

As we also mentioned in chapter 1, the United States federal government decided to, for the first time, recognize LGBT marriages. Since then, we have witnessed some rather disturbing public scapegoating of the LGBT community, primarily carried out by more fundamentalist, right-wing Christians.[27] For an example, consider what *The 700 Club* host Pat Robertson said vis-à-vis gay marriage. After likening LGBT people with the "virulent homosexuals"[28] who attempted to rape the angels in the Sodom story (found in Gen 19), Robertson states, "I warned about this years and years ago that it was going to happen and it did, it has. What's next? What's next is what happened to Sodom and Gomorrah. It is just a question of how soon the wrath of God is going to come on this land."[29] In a case of classic scapegoating, the LGBT community, according to Robertson, will likely be to "blame" for whatever he in the future deems as the "wrath of God." Of course, this "wrath" will no doubt come in the form of a future tornado, hurricane, earthquake, or even human violence. Just ask the Westboro Baptist Church.

If only we could rid ourselves of the LGBT community, then we could have peace and be spared from "the wrath of God."

As if there wasn't enough wrong with Robertson's monologue, when Robertson suggests that the "sins of Sodom" is akin to "virulent homosexuality," he is actually promoting a blatant falsehood. As Robertson must no doubt be privy to, in Ezekiel 16:49, *the Bible clearly states* that the sins of Sodom were pride, an excess of food, and a lack of concern for the poor and needy. They were not, as Robertson so ineloquently puts it, sins specific to "virulent homosexuals."[30] You see, a key part of scapegoating is the dissemination of false information, slander, and gossip. Robertson's remarks most assuredly fall into all three of these categories.

Now, before we move on to our final real-world example of scapegoating, I want to introduce you to my friend, Brian Cordova, who has *tacit*—or in other words experiential—knowledge of this specific type of LGBT scapegoating.

> During the sixties and seventies, I grew up in two different cities in Texas. The first part of my youth was spent in Abilene. Then, when I was eight, my family moved to Fort Worth. Now, we were not the best churchgoers, but if we *were* anything, it was Southern Baptist. This fact about me will be important to keep in mind.

> You see, I always knew that I was "different," but could not place my finger on what this difference was. I had always heard that "boys like girls" and, subsequently, "girls like boys." Yet, as a small child, I was also taught to look out for "funny men," as they were unaffectionately called. As I got a little older, I began to hear different words used; words like "queer" and "fag." At first, I did not know what these terms meant. So, I did what any boy would do, I asked an older sibling. And what I would discover would change everything.

If I may be frank, what those terms truly described was exactly what I was: homosexual. And it did not appear to be something very highly regarded. Before long, I began to develop a sense of fear and shame. My "inner secret" haunted me throughout my teenage years. I wondered if I was the only one (or at least, the only one in Fort Worth) who felt this way. It was a most isolating feeling.

As the years went by, I became more troubled by not only the "hellfire and damnation" messages of my Southern Baptist upbringing, but also their complete animosity toward homosexuals. It was obvious that their unity was due, in part, to having a common "enemy." This was enflamed by Anita Bryant's holy war against the gay community, as scores of "good, godly people"—including some of my immediate family—defended her crusade.

All this time, I knew that my orientation was not a choice, yet it appeared as if God condemned me anyway. When I had my first crushes, for instance, they were all-the-more painful, because, not only could I not speak to anyone of them; but fear, guilt, and shame overtook me because of their being male. I knew that if any of them were to discover my secret, I would be considered a "predator." It should be no surprise then, as to why I would experience some of the worst depression of my life and even entertained suicidal thoughts during these years.

What this brings me to is the crux of what I have to say. Which is, instead of being met with empathy and compassion, people like me—i.e., gay—who have gone through similar things, are often met with accusations and condemnation.

Allow me to offer an example of what I mean.

One of the most difficult things I have ever witnessed because of hatred like this was the overall response—spearheaded by the Reagan family—in the eighties and nineties to those inflicted with AIDS within the gay male population. I can clearly remember that throughout "Christian" radio and television, the advice given was not so much to act as Jesus would, but simply to "get 'them' out of our faces!" Clearly, the collective and unified voice of the accuser rang loud during these darkest of days. Without a doubt, the strongest opponents against any form of protection for the LGBT community, as well as assistance for gay men suffering with AIDS, were those who labeled themselves as "Christian."[31]

Now, let's look at one final example of scapegoating, as it is a current one, before moving on to what Girard calls "the pillars of culture."

THE MUSLIM COMMUNITY SINCE 2015

If you live in the United States and are Muslim, or even if you stand in solidarity with those of the Muslim faith—especially if you are a Christian like myself—then you are probably aware that, depending on where you live and/or travel, you need to "tread lightly." That is because, as it currently stands, Muslims are not really welcomed by many here in the United States. Take, for instance, the recent near-incident outside of a Texas mosque. After the 2015 terrorist attacks in Paris—attacks the mosque "strongly condemned," saying "they have absolutely no basis in the religion on [sic] Islam"[32]—heavily armed protestors stood outside the worship center with signs that contained violent rhetoric, such as: "Stop the Islamization of America."[33] This is not surprising as, according to recent FBI statistics, violence against Muslims is on the *rise*, in spite of the fact that hate crimes based on religious beliefs is on the *decline* overall.[34]

Just listen to the rhetoric that helps trigger cultural shifts like this—the subtle scapegoating in some cases—from some US politicians and Christian faith leaders:

> If there's a rabid dog running around in your neighborhood, you're probably not going to assume something good about that dog, and you're probably going to put your children out of the

way. It doesn't mean that you hate all dogs by any stretch of the imagination, but you're putting your intellect into motion.[35] (Ben Carson)

They're [the Syrian refugees] going to be gone. They will go back...I've said it before, in fact, and everyone hears what I say, including them, believe it or not. But if they're here, they have to go back, because we cannot take a chance. You look at the migration; it's young, strong men.[36] We cannot take a chance that the people coming over here are going to be ISIS-affiliated... We're going to have to do things that we never did before. And some people are going to be upset about it, but I think that now everybody is feeling that security is going to rule. And certain things will be done that we never thought would happen in this country in terms of information and learning about the enemy. And so we're going to have to do certain things that were frankly unthinkable a year ago.[37] (Donald Trump)

We're not dealing with a religion. People say, "Oh, it's just terrible, you shouldn't discriminate one religion versus the other." Well, yes you can if one religion is actually a political system that is intent on dominating you and killing you. Christianity isn't intent on dominating you and killing you, it just isn't.[38] (Pat Robertson)

What one should notice about all three statements (and those similar), is that all, in one way or another, liken Muslims to "potential terrorists." Rather predictably, given the fact that all three gentlemen quoted are proclaimed "Christians," neither Carson, Trump, nor Robertson even seem willing (at least publicly per my research) to admit Christians carry this same potential, in spite of such groups as the Klu Klux Klan, and South Carolina gunman Dylann Roof, et al. And when a culture uses dissimilar language to define similar behaviors between different ethnic and religious groups, then that is a tell-tale sign that it is in the midst of scapegoating.[39] This sure seems like the case here.

If only we could rid ourselves of Muslims, then we could be safe, "have our country back," and be made "great again."

Our journey throughout this chapter has taken us from the way in which human beings learn and desire (through mimesis), to how this mimetic desire then leads to rivalry, violence, and subsequent scapegoating. Let us conclude with how ancient cultures and religions were formed around these fundamentally human behaviors. Then, we will begin to have an appropriate anthropological context for the Bible.

THE FOUNDATIONS OF CULTURE AND RELIGION

In *All Set Free*, I laid out what Girard called the "three pillars of culture"—prohibition, ritual, and myth—that is to say, the three "ingredients" needed for humans to structure society, and avoid getting back to a place of unmediated violence. We will revisit that discussion here as it directly relates to how the scapegoated victim—the "cause" of all the problems in the first place—is then sacralized and sometimes even deified by the community. In other words, our victims eventually often become gods.

PROHIBITION

We start here, with prohibitions, because prohibitions are most closely associated with what caused a society's strife to begin with, or as Michael Hardin points out, "it is more intimately associated with the 'originary event.'"[40] *So what are these prohibitions and why do we have them?* Well, most carnally, the first prohibitions, as Hardin points out, were centered on food and women. "Our earliest human taboos relate to sex and hunger, two natural instincts now being controlled by prohibition."[41]

Don't take my woman and don't touch my plate!

What happens is that a community will center on a kill from the hunt, let's say, and while hunger will cause them to indeed desire the food the animal provides, an immense increase in desire happens simply because they all desire it and all unconsciously take notice of this (*mimesis*). As we discussed earlier, this potentially then leads us down the path of mimetic rivalry and violence.

"I want that cut of meat!"

"No, I do!"

When this happens, the community can look back and realize that prohibitions of specific items are needed, so as to attempt to prevent *this sort of thing from happening again*. From there, the specific behaviors and even the certain characteristics of others that are *believed* to have led to the rivalrous contagion—historically twins, adolescents, and women during menstruation—are prohibited as well.[42] This is because, as Girard notes, prohibitions are antimimetic in nature.[43]

This is why we find so many "odd" prohibitions in a place like Torah. At least, many of us tend to think of them as "odd" now. We read of laws against eating certain types of animals, prohibitions on sexual orientations, and on various fabrics and hairstyles. And we cannot quite grasp why God seemed to care so much about all of that stuff. To that, I would say, "he really didn't." These were in place because they had to do with some original conflict that arose because of the prohibited item or behavior; at least, what is recognized by those placing the various prohibitions.

To sum up: because prohibitions are the group's attempt to look back upon the thing, behavior, and type of distinguishing trait that led to the communal violence in the first place, we then conclude that their goal is in fact peace. As Girard emphasizes, "There is no culture that does not prohibit violence among those who live together. All occasions or events that might give rise to real violence...are prohibited."[44] This includes the ancient Jewish people. But, as I mentioned, these prohibitions do require the mimetic conflict that led to the killing of that developing culture's surrogate victim in the first place. Simply put: prohibitions presuppose violence. James Alison sums this thought up in the following: "This means that social prohibition is essentially a violent form of protection against violence, made possible by a murder."[45]

One final note on prohibitions: while they often succeed in quelling unmediated violence, they will also cause desire for the prohibited "thing" to increase and become "twisted," so to speak. This only perpetuates the cyclical nature of this phenomenon, which is the very thing they are attempting to avoid. Thus, they are paradoxical. We have all witnessed this any time we tell a child he or she cannot do something or have something—and everyone knows what happens when we are told not to "press the red button." *We've just gotta push that button!* Thus, to quell violence, we cannot simply end at prohibitions.

RITUAL

When ancient humans noticed that their collective violence, poured onto one victim, worked as a means to achieve peace, albeit temporary, their conclusion was that their behavior was ordained by the divine. Inevitably though, this "divinely ordained" peace would again turn to violence due to our innate mimetic desire (and after the prohibitions that the community placed inevitably fail). To accommodate, they would need to reenact the original killing, this time on a new victim, in hopes that what worked before would work again. And so, *ritual* is born.

What do these rituals look like?

Well, each culture or religion's rites would be different. Whereas the prohibitions that cultures place are antimimetic, rituals reenact the mimetic crisis that led to the killing of the scapegoat. They also reenact the killing, which is why this violence is sacred. James Alison explains it this way: "We must repeat, insofar as possible, the original expulsion which led to our peace. So we produce a rite which consists of a well-controlled mime of an act of mass-violence which ends in the immolation of some victim, originally human, later animal, and so on."[46]

Sacrifice

Although Girard acknowledges that there are in fact rituals that do not *always* lead to the sacrifice of another (either human or animal), he also states: "The conclusion of a ritual might be limited to ritual mutilation or to exorcism, but these are always the equivalent of sacrifice."[47] That is to say, these violent actions *represent* the original sacrifice.

Throughout history, we find compelling evidence of this practice, which can be performed with just a few piles of rocks on top of a mountain, or in a temple like the one in the Second Temple Jewish system of Jesus' day (which we will discuss in chapter 5). The first piece of evidence to examine at this point, however, is from thousands of years prior to Jesus, from a place called Göbekli Tepe (located in the Southeastern Anatolia Region of Turkey). This site is believed by some to be humanity's most ancient (possibly around the tenth-millennium BCE). In Antonello Pierpaolo and Paul Gifford's essay, "Rethinking the Neolithic Revolution," after mentioning that the site's pillars *could have been* used for passage rites and that the human bones found there show evidence of "ritualistic manipulation,"[48] they offer the following:

"The representation of a headless human with erect penis is recognizable quite clearly. The state of the man could indicate a violent death, and his company of scorpions, snakes, and vultures strengthens this impression."[49] We note also other images consistent with this interpretation: a boar, splayed out upside down with its feet in the air (on the rim of one of the pothole stones); or the image of the vulture grasping in its claws two severed human heads. The design and layout of what Schmidt calls the circles or the enclosures of this temple complex are also highly revealing, particularly in light of Girard's theory. The circles separate the sacred and the profane spheres, both excluding the mass of the pilgrims, who are relegated to the role of spectators standing on the earthen ramps beyond the outer perimeter, yet at the same time engaging the participation of all, as suggested by the human-like T-stones facing inwards towards the center, perhaps representing ritual representatives (shamans or early priests) in whom the crowd find their own drama expressed and through whose actions it is played out—representatives who, perhaps in the order of ritual precedence, as marked by their iconographic insignia of animal images, advance into the third, second, or first ranked circle, leaving the innermost circle to the victim, who is both most intensely identified with and, at the same time, done to death sacrificially.[50]

I do realize that this is but one interpretation of the site. Indeed, not all archaeologists accept it and we are in no place to take too strong a stance. What we can say, however, is that even if Göbekli Tepe is not to be interpreted as an *official* ritual site, it does at least point in that direction. In other words, this site points to a future practice that would be central in how culture and religion is formed and maintained. Another such site that comes to mind is Çatalhöyük (7500 BCE–5700 BCE). From the perspective of the mimetic theory, the paintings discovered at this site—depicting sacrificial animals surrounded by large groups of people, predominantly men—tell us what was deemed sacred by our earliest ancestors; namely, the communal killing of a sacrificial victim.

Now, these are just two instances where there is strong evidence of a sacrificial religious system centered specifically on human sacrifice. There are plenty of others. Possibly the one we are most familiar with, as it was in practice all the way up until the sixteenth century, is that of the Aztecs. Some, such as historical anthropologist Ross Hassig, estimate that somewhere between 10,000 and 80,000 prisoners were sacrificed during one four-day ceremony.[51] The efficiency of numbers like that may even rival places like Auschwitz-Birkenau but because, in the minds of the people, it's what "pleased the gods," it had to be done. (We should note that some Nazis believed this as well.) If it were not, chaos and disorder would ensue as the gods would no doubt remove their blessing.

Understanding where the practice of sacrifice originates from will be vital for anyone who wants to approach the Hebrew and Christian Scriptures. This sacred violence that we have been exploring will be a point of contention throughout the Hebrew Scriptures, and even outright denounced by later prophets. And, for Christians most specifically, sacrifice will be central in how we understand Jesus—his teachings, his relationship with the Father, and how he "atones" for sins. For now, let us move on to how communities shape their stories, their "history," or in other words, their *mythology*.

MYTHOLOGY

We have now arrived at a crucial question: *How are we, as the community who just went through a (non-conscious) mimetic crisis, only to resolve it by pouring our collective violence unto a scapegoat, going to tell the story?* First, we certainly are not going to tell it as if we, the community, are guilty. Guilt has to be attributed to the victim, the one we had to destroy in order for the "whole" to be spared. And that is the key to understanding myth, it tells the story as if the victim is guilty of the community's accusations. This understanding of myth, where it is the great deceiver, is different than theologian Rudolf Bultmann's, which suggests myth is simply how stories are formed in a pre-scientific age.[52] For Girard, myth is more. Myth is the papering over of the truth of how we create unity through the use of violence.

Moreover, as evidenced at Göbekli Tepe, the destruction of the victim is often not even attributed to the community, but rather, to the gods (or God). *Our violence is divine violence.* This ideology is further evidenced in Claude Lévi-Strauss' *Totemism* which Girard uses in his work, *Things Hidden Since the Foundation of the World.*[53] The myth is from the Ojibwa Indians and is as follows:

> The five "original" clans are descended from six anthropomorphic supernatural beings who emerged from the ocean to mingle with human beings. One of them had his eyes covered and dared not look at the Indians, though he showed the greatest anxiety to do so. At last he could no longer restrain his curiosity, and on one occasion he partially lifted his veil, and his eye fell on the form of a human being, who instantly fell dead "as if struck by one of the thunderers." Though the intentions of this dread being were friendly to men, yet the glance of his eye was too strong, and it inflicted certain death. His fellows therefore caused him to return to the bosom of the great water. The five others remained among the Indians, and "became a blessing to them." From them originate the five great clans or totems.[54]

Girard exegetes this story in the following way: "The noxious effects of the crisis are immediately attributed to the victim, who, as always, appears to be responsible for them. In the… myth the sudden death of an Indian is supposedly caused by the simple gaze of the future victim."[55] Again, blame rests not with the community, but on a future victim.

Myth after myth, "with God on our side," the victim is either killed like the unnamed person in the above story or like the god Tezcatlipoca,[56] or expelled like in the Tikopia myth, where a god named Tikarau is driven away from the other gods after a "trial of strength and speed."[57] While contours of the stories are slightly different, the moral implication in each is the same: "*he*" *was the problem and had to go!*

Now, before moving on to the sacralization of the victim, I wanted to mention one tale from the Bible where this plays out. I will do this so that when I later say "the Bible parallels myth to subvert myth," it will make much more sense. This particular story comes from Num 25. In this myth, a great plague falls over Israel. The cause, you might ask? God's anger is said to be "kindled against Israel" because some of the Israelites began having sex with Midianite women, and thus began worshiping their gods. So the only natural thing to do for the Israelite leaders was to expel those who are "causing" the plague. The "hero" who carries this out is a man named Phinehas. Num 25:6–8 gives the account:

> Just then one of the Israelites came and brought a Midianite woman into his family, in the sight of Moses and in the sight of the whole congregation of the Israelites, while they were weeping at the entrance of the tent and meeting. When Phinehas son of Eleazar, son of Aaron the priest, saw it, he got up and left the congregation. Taking a spear in his hand, he went after the Israelite man into the tent, and pierced the two of them, the Israelite and the woman, through the belly.

Notice how, in Num 25:8, the plague is said to immediately cease. Once the scapegoat is expelled, peace ensues. And so, Phinehas receives a "covenant of peace," as well as a "covenant of perpetual priesthood" (Num 25:12–13). You read that correctly! For killing an interracial couple, Phinehas is given a covenant of *peace*. To be blunt: that is mythology, where we write the account as if the victims expelled are bad and the victimizers are good, pure, holy, righteous, etc.

THE SACRALIZATION OF THE VICTIM

The final thing we need to discuss before concluding this chapter is what is known as the "sacralization of the victim." What is meant by this is that often, but not always, myths attribute god-like status to the surrogate victims. That is because the victim, although indeed believed to be the cause of the community's troubles, is now seen as the bringer of peace; he is then viewed as divine in origin. He must be or else his killing would not have appeased the gods. So the victim becomes sacralized and even often deified: one of the gods. He will become the center of the community's praise, idols will be made in his name, and they will institute rituals that repeat the communal bloodletting.

From "guilty" victim to god…

For one such example of how this plays out, take the myth of King Oedipus. In this tale, an Oracle of the god Apollo prophesied that Oedipus would one day kill his father and marry his mother. To prevent this, Oedipus' royal parents (King Laius and Queen Jocasta of Thebes) decide to murder the young boy. However, Oedipus is rescued by some shepherds of King Polybus and Queen Merope. This king and queen then raise Oedipus as their own son.

When Oedipus is older, he learns about the prophecy and in order to save who he believes are his real parents flees for the city of Thebes. While on his journey, Oedipus gets into a fight with a stranger and kills him. Later, he learns that the king of Thebes (his real father) is deceased and that a sphinx is holding the city captive. So what does Oedipus do? He solves the riddle and frees the city from the sphinx's grasp. As a reward, Oedipus is made king of Thebes.

After some time, Oedipus learns the truth about who the stranger that he slew was. It was none other than his real father, King Laius of Thebes. And that meant that when King Oedipus took the throne, he in fact married his very own mother, Queen Jocasta, just as the Oracle prophesied.

I want us to pay special attention to what happens next: Apollo sends a plague on Thebes that forces them to expel King Oedipus. Once Oedipus is removed from the city, peace ensues, the plague is gone. And that is just what mythology states. The expelled victim is guilty (Oedipus) and his removal brings peace (the end of the Apollonian plague). And Oedipus is then depicted as a hero of sorts. Sure, he is a tragic hero, but he is a hero nonetheless. After all, he was a king. He was the savior of Thebes not once, but twice, first from the Sphinx and then by his expulsion at the end of the story. And so, he is sacralized, forever as King Oedipus, the tragic savior of Thebes.

If these gods we create are not only products of violence (and they are), but that they in fact mandate sacred violence (which they do), then as creatures of imitation, we will most assuredly follow suit. This is a dangerous notion as we will always need more victims if we are going to carry out "the will of the gods." And that is why we will attempt to make the case that, while including the voices of those who do victimize in God's name, the Bible does progress us away from such a belief about God. If we do not see this, then what tangible good would the Bible be for us in this violent world? Because of what we discussed in chapter 1, a lack of a solution to these problems is not a good thing.

That being said, it is my contention that the Bible does offer a solution: The Gospels. And while the way in which that story is told *resembles* just another story of the sacralization process, there will be distinct differences that clue us into the fact that something else is going on. For now, we will leave that discussion for chapter 5.

IN CLOSING

Through our overview of the mimetic theory developed by René Girard, what we have attempted to point out is how mimetic desire is at the center of why there is such a propensity toward human violence. We touched on the theory from a psychological perspective, an anthropological one, as well as drawing evidence from the realm of archaeology.[58] We also discussed what Girard labeled as "the three pillars of culture"—prohibition, ritual, and myth—and explored how each of them structure our societies. Understanding all of this will be a key component to under-standing much of the anthropology of the Scriptures.

Before we begin our discussion on the specifics of the bibli-cal solution to this problem, we need to investigate the work of another cultural anthropologist, Ernest Becker, who has a different take than Girard on the problem of human violence. Whereas Girard posits that it is our mimetic desire that is the cause, Becker argues that it is our anxiety over our own future demise that drives us to such a profound problem. In spite of this difference, however, the work of both men can easily go hand in hand, and rather than contradicting each other, they actually complement one another.

CHAPTER 3

ROOT CAUSE #2: DEATH ANXIETY

"Of all things that move man, one of the principal ones is his terror of death."[1]

–ERNEST BECKER

Ernest Becker (September 27, 1924–March 6, 1974) was a Jewish-American cultural anthropologist from Springfield, Massachusetts. As a young adult, and prior to his academic career, he joined the military, where, during one of his missions, he liberated those trapped in a Nazi concentration camp.[2] After his return, he attended Syracuse University, earning his PhD in the spring of 1960. From there, Becker went on to teach anthropology at the Upstate Medical Center in Syracuse and then later, beginning in 1969, at Simon Fraser University in Vancouver, British Columbia. It is during this time where he would publish his greatest work, the Pulitzer Prize-winning *The Denial of Death*. Sadly, shortly after this masterpiece was published, Becker died from colon cancer at the age of forty-nine.

Since Becker's death, the *Ernest Becker Foundation* has been founded. One of the primary goals of the organization, according to their mission statement, is to use the work of Ernest

Becker to educate others in hopes of fostering "a healthier and more peaceful world."[3] In 2003, the Foundation even assisted in funding a documentary entitled *Flight from Death: the Quest for Immortality*, which won multiple awards and accolades, including "Best Documentary" at the Rhode Island International Film Festival.

Now, before we delve into Becker's work on death anxiety specifically, we need to have a working knowledge about how humans—the self-conscious beings that we are—think abstractly about death. This is because, and as I mentioned in the previous chapter, it is in our ability to symbolically ponder our own mortality that is at the heart of our violence problem. And while this is different than what Girard posits, I tend to think the truth of the matter is that it is not a case of "either/or," but "both/and."

SELF CONSCIOUSNESS

Humans are unique in that we can use the pronoun "I" to describe ourselves. My best friend Mike calls this the symbolic self, as it is but a symbol of what truly is. Now, because of this ability to create symbolism, we can create all sorts of magic— i.e., great works of art, music, and literature.[4] However, the ability to symbolize also creates quite a conundrum. We also carry with us the ability to ponder our mortality. And that is what lies at the heart of the issue.

THE KNOWLEDGE OF DEATH

The knowledge of our impending doom is a uniquely human characteristic. Becker elucidates the difference between humans and the lower animals in the following:

Man is literally split in two: he has an awareness of his own splendid uniqueness in that he sticks out of nature with a towering majesty, and yet he goes back into the ground a few feet in order blindly and dumbly to rot and disappear forever. It is a terrifying dilemma to be in and to have to live with. The lower animals are, of course, spared this painful contradiction, as they lack a symbolic identity and the self-consciousness that goes with it. They merely act and move reflexively as they are driven by their instincts.[5]

To put it another way, Becker, drawing from the work of Danish philosopher Søren Kierkegaard, explains the difference thusly:

Man is a union of opposites, of self-consciousness and of physical body. Man emerged from the instinctive thoughtless action of the lower animals and came to reflect on his condition. He was given a consciousness of his individuality and his part-divinity in creation, the beauty and uniqueness of his face and his name. At the same time he was given the consciousness of the terror of the world and of his own death and decay.[6]

So, what precisely does this knowledge of death do to a person?

To answer that question, we must first make mention of what Becker calls "heroism." Then we will be able to better understand why our knowledge of death causes such an anxiety within our fragile, yet "heroic," self.

THE HERO IN US ALL

Essential to understanding the human propensity toward heroism is recognizing that at its core heroism is completely narcissistic.[7] That is to say, humans are self-centered. As we are all no doubt aware, the desire to have self-worth, self-esteem, self-this and self-that, is paramount to our happiness. And so to validate this understanding of the self, one must think of themself as a hero, something more than they really are.

We witness the most obvious form of self-centered behavior in children (although the narcissism displayed by adults can be just as palpable at times). This is not to say that the child is bad but simply that he is less filtered. He clamors about being first to eat, first through a doorway, and first to receive a treat. He must have the biggest slice of cake, or at least the one with the most frosting. He boldly yells, "Look at me!" every time he has a new trick to show off. In short, the child is the center of the universe. Actually, if we look through our Girardian lens for a moment, we will recognize that *every child* must be the center of the universe as they no doubt imitate each other in this self-aggrandizing behavior. Therefore, *all* of the children clamor about being first to eat, first through a doorway, and first to receive a treat. They must all have the biggest slice of cake, or at least the one with the most frosting. They all boldly yell, "Look at me!"

While this behavior is most obvious in children, it is present in adults as well. Perhaps as we get older, we become more subtle or calculating in our narcissistic behavior, but we tend to always retain this certain idea of the self.

DEATH ANXIETY

The idea of the self is so powerful—often thought to even be 100 percent crucial to the order of the cosmos—that death must, somehow, be something we conquer in order to remain sane. If it is not—if our knowledge of our own death is something that cannot be triumphed over—then our ever-so-inflated narcissistic self could not handle it. That is to say, we could have a psychotic break. Becker offers multiple examples of this in chapter 10 of *The Denial of Death*, specifically explaining how depression, schizophrenia, and sexual perversion can arise from our being overcome by neurotic death anxiety.[8]

And I can attest to this. All throughout my youth, I lived with this inability to repress my anxiety over death, and so, experienced all of the symptoms of PTSD—intrusive memories, avoidance, negative changes in mood, and changes in emotional reactions. The most memorable anxiety-ridden events, though, were the night terrors, sleep paralysis, and countless recurrent nightmares (which, as Becker points out, is a telltale sign that a child is processing their terror of death[9]). I want to share a few of these.

Spiders, Scorpions, and Snakes Oh My!

The setting was familiar. It was after hours in a local department store, which was almost completely dark, save for a few dim lights in the distance. These were not regular lights though. Their tinge was dark orange, most definitely the glow from a fire of some sort. Because this dream had happened before, I knew the terror that would be coming my way. However, fear kept me stuck in place, fixated on the distant blaze. Then it would happen like every time before, where from out of the inferno, endless crawling creatures; *spiders*, *scorpions*, and *snakes*. Regardless of how hard I tried, no matter how fast I thought I was, I could not outrun the hellish beings. Inevitably, I found myself overwhelmed.

Thankfully, that is when I would always wake up. Often, though, I would be drenched in sweat, my heart pounding out of my boyish chest. Sleep, at least for the nearest foreseeable future, would be impossible. Eventually though, I *would* have to find it again. But laying my head back onto my pillow meant not knowing if I would find myself right back where I started, staring into the orange glow of what must have been "hell." Yet, to sleep I would go, to face the monsters that haunted my young, fragile mind.

Armageddon

Another horrifying and recurrent nightmare I had was an "Armageddon-esque" battle, right out of the book of Revelation.[10] At my side on every occasion was my dear grandfather, Leonard. He was one of a handful of childhood heroes of mine. I looked up to him in nearly every way and to use Girardian language, he was most assuredly a model of *positive mimesis*. However, he also seemed very agnostic about matters of faith. He would rarely, if ever, talk about anything related to God. It just did not seem all that important to him. This terrified me because I was theologically an Arminian,[11] and to my knowledge, my grandfather had never "freely chosen" Jesus Christ as his "personal Lord and Savior" (a phrase not once found in Scripture). I believe this is the predominant reason as to why he was always with me in the war created by my mind.

I cannot recall how often my grandfather was killed in my dreams. The only thing I can remember is that, on at least a few occasions, I had to carry his dead body through the killing fields. This was unbearable and again, my sleep would often be interrupted by this all too familiar event.

It was madness!

"Snake Eyes!"

The above dreams are just two examples of the many nightmarish memories that I carry with me from my youth. Yet another is recalling the night where I ran throughout my house—half asleep, half awake, and screaming "Snake eyes!" at the top of my lungs. Nothing was recognizable, not even my own parents. I cannot recall the visuals that I may have had during this event, but to this day, my mother is convinced I was demon-possessed. I would not disagree with her; although would understand my demons ontologically different than her, naming them *pavor nocturnes*, or "night terrors." Regardless of one's definition of "demon," what I experienced was truly demonic—a mind possessed by what I believed at that time to be an absolute truth. That supposed truth? Most humans were destined to a place my dreams could only allude to, a place we call "hell."

THE DENIAL OF DEATH

Humans cannot function properly if they are mentally plagued in this manner. As I said above, death must, somehow, be something we conquer in order to remain sane. So how do we do this?

First, we do what we can to repress the thought of death. For some of us, we try to get lost in the world around us, try to live in the moment, the here and now. And that is a good thing. However, the manageable world we attempt to live in is not always so easy to manage. Eventually death will find a way to one's doorstep. Perhaps a diagnosis of cancer or near-fatal car accident will do the trick. And if not that, then simply age itself will. The body will begin to decay at some point, and when it does, we reticently realize escape is futile. Becker writes:

> At times like this, when the awareness dawns that has always been blotted out by frenetic, ready-made activity, we see the transmutation of repression redistilled, so to speak, and the fear of death emerges in pure essence...when repression no longer works...forward momentum of activity is no longer possible."[12]

Because repressing death does not "work" entirely, we must have something much more lasting, much more meaningful. We, as self-declared "heroes," must live on after our bodily demise. So we create what Becker calls "immortality systems," or in other words, belief systems that make certain of one's own immortality. That is to say, we create such things as religions, cultures, sects, and political ideologies in order to "guarantee" that death—at least symbolically—shall never come. As we will discover, we must then defend (even unto death if we must) these systems that protect our self—the "hero" of the cosmos.

DEFENSE OF THE IMMORTALITY SYSTEM

When we identify with one particular culture, religion, or political ideology, we have potentially—nay, most likely—set ourselves up against all others. Because our systems are such that they "guarantee" our immortality, we must view them as an absolute and immutable truth. If not, then everything we have constructed in order to protect our own immortality may come tumbling down like a house of cards. *What we believe is truth with a capital T—a "God-given" truth even!* And when another Truth system comes in play, each system must be defended by their respective adherents. Philosopher Glenn Hughes explains:

> We have to protect ourselves against the exposure of our absolute truth being just one more mortality-denying system among others, which we can only do by insisting that all other absolute truths are false. So we attack and degrade—preferably kill—the adherents of different mortality-denying-absolute-truth systems. So the Protestants kill the Catholics; the Muslims vilify the Christians and vice versa; upholders of the American way of life denounce Communists; the Communist Khmer Rouge slaughters all the intellectuals in Cambodia; the Spanish Inquisition tortures heretics; and all good students of the Enlightenment demonize religion as the source of all evil. The list could go on and on.[13]

Indeed, the list does go on and on.

Just notice how it is the most rigidly fundamentalist of folks who commit acts of violence in their immortality system's name. It is not the mystical Sufi who straps a bomb to his torso, blowing up hundreds of people. It is the fundamentalist Muslim who does this in the name of Allah. It is not the Franciscan Father who praises the Westboro Baptist Church prior to shooting up a black congregation. It is the fundamentalist Christian who does this in the name of Jesus. It is not the Buddhist monk who shoots the world's most famous Hindu peace activist. It is the member of the fundamentalist Hindu Mahasabha (Hindu nationalist political party in India). And on and on it goes. Many of the people listed above, and then also some who are not, feel that the defending of their ideology and position is a matter of life and death—sadly, often literally so.

CONCLUDING THOUGHTS

Over the course of our journey so far, we have attempted to make the case that violence is humanity's greatest problem, offering evidence from various epochs in human history, and showing that violence transcends cultures and religions.

Also, we explored two potential root causes for our inherent problem, namely mimetic desire (Girard) and death anxiety (Becker). The goal in doing this was to build a foundation from which we can move forward toward our solution—because you cannot treat a disease without a correct diagnosis. The past two chapters, then, was our working toward a proper diagnosis.

The remainder of the book, beginning with a pilgrimage into the Hebrew Bible, is the perfect cure. Now, rather than viewing the Jewish Scriptures as an outdated and antiquated book (as post-Enlightenment atheists do), or as the inerrant and infallible Word of God (as conservative fundamentalists do), we will attempt to put aside all presuppositions for a moment and open up our minds to see if, perhaps, there is something entirely different going on there. I believe that there indeed is and will attempt to show just how revelatory and progressive the Hebrew

Scriptures truly are, in spite of the archaic religiosity that is present as well. So, let us fasten our seatbelts and dive headlong into the Scriptures, as it is there where I believe that we will discover a theological-anthropological solution to the human problem of violence.

PART II
THE SOLUTION

THE HEBREW SCRIPTURES: RELIGION, REVELATION, AND DISCERNING THE DIFFERENCE

"In the Hebrew Bible, there is clearly a dynamic that moves in the direction of the rehabilitation of the victims, but it is not a cut-and-dried thing. Rather, it is a process under way, a text in travail…a struggle that advances and retreats." [1]

—RENÉ GIRARD

The Bible is approached in many different ways by many different people. For some, it is nothing but fairy tales and mythology, an ancient relic better fit for the Smithsonian than the halls of Congress. For others, it is the other way around. It is the rulebook of life, the giver of law, the unblemished Word of God. But what if the Bible is something different than these altogether? What if it actually is a collection of works—with blemishes included—that engage the reality of humanity's plight? For the Girardian, it would be the problem of sin and death, where sin originates due to our twisted mimetic desire, which then leads to violence and death. For the Beckerian, it is death that leads to sin and violence.[2] Or, as the writer of Hebrews put it, we are slaves to the fear of death (Heb 2:15)—our sin bondage stemming from our bondage to death anxiety.[3] No matter how we slice it—whether sin leads to death (Protestant) or death leads to sin (Orthodox)—sin and death are intertwined, the plight is all of humanity's, and all of humanity needs salvation.

And speaking of salvation, our ultimate destination in the second half of our journey will be Jesus Christ and the Gospels. But we will have to begin in the Hebrew Bible, in what Christians often call the "Old Testament." In these Scriptures, we will see how revelation (an unveiling) *begins* to poke holes in the veil of sacred violence (religion), where glimpses of a non-retributive, all-merciful, all-loving, Christlike God can be seen in spite of all of the sinfully violent, victim-inducing human projections we and our immortality systems have placed onto him. These will be but glimpses though, as these Scriptures *will* share similarities with other sacred texts, and contain plenty of mythology throughout (Remember, myth often justifies violence committed against others.)[4] It is, as Girard often discussed, a text in travail.

However, in spite of this, there will be stories that emerge that challenge the religious paradigm. There will be anthropological and psychological revelations, as well as theological ones. We will cover topics such as mimetic desire and sacrifice, as well as introducing something *not* found in mythology, namely the voice of the victim. This will then hopefully pave the way for the ultimate paradigm shift we discover in the Gospels, where God reveals himself through his son, who is portrayed as truly innocent while the community is portrayed as guilty. In this respect, the voice of the victim will speak the word of peace, and will unveil the ultimate anthropological-theological shift. First, we will start with Gen 1:1, where we begin to encounter this counter-narrative.

REVELATION ONE: CREATION WITHOUT VIOLENCE (GEN 1:1-2:3)

There are countless ancient creation myths that center on divine violence. Gods are so often deceptive, ruthless, vindictive, and down-right bloodthirsty. In *All Set Free*, I summed up one such account, *Enuma Elish*, the Babylonian version of how this world came to be, in the following way:

> Two primordial gods, Apsu and Tiamat, engage in a sexual union and give birth to multiple generations of gods who begin to torment Tiamat with their incessant noise. Apsu and Tiamat plan to kill their sons but Ea (the water god) foils their plan and kills Apsu. Ea hires a hero named Marduk, who is given divine powers in order to defeat Tiamat. He defeats Tiamat and uses half of her body to create the heavens and half to create the earth. The blood of Tiamat's commander, Kingu, is used to create mankind.[5]

A similar tale is that of the *Mandé* creation myth, where our planet is a bi-product of deception, where in which the blood of a scapegoat (Faro) is used to purify an earth that was impure due to Pemba's desire for power. And then there is the *Tungusic* creation myth, where the creator god Buga defeats a devilish character named Buninka. It is only after winning a challenge and after painfully turning Buninka's head to iron that Buga creates humankind. There are many more tales that tell of a world created after the spilling of divine blood, with humanity created as an after-thought and only after violence was present.

Now, when we turn to the Hebrew version of creation, we should notice that none of this violent back-story is present. Instead, in the beginning, God spoke. He speaks things into a "formless void."[6] Some, like Jewish rabbi Isaac Luria, use the term *tzimtzum* to describe the empty space where God's infinite light poured in.[7] Either way, from out of the "primordial waters," the writer poetically tells us that God simply wills creation into existence. In fact, as my friend Mark Stone once pointed out to me, not only is creation metaphysically non-violent, but even the Hebrew grammar of the text is in the non-violent jussive mood—"Let there be light"—as opposed to the coercive imperative: "Shine, light!"

Simplicity then gives way to more and more complex creations. From the formation of day and night in Gen 1:5 all the way to fish, birds, and mammals in vv. 20–25. Finally, in a wonderfully relational way, in comes humanity in vv. 26–27, which read:

> Then God said, 'Let us make humankind in our image, according to our likeness; and let them have dominion over the fish of the sea, and over the birds of the air, and over the cattle, and over all the wild animals of the earth, and over every creeping thing that creeps upon the earth.' So God created humankind in his image, in the image of God he created them; male and female he created them.

If we look closely, we can see evidence of the interdividuality of humankind that Girard introduces us to. We see that God's image is relational, both "male and female." Humanity, or *adam* in Hebrew, is both man and woman, not simply man. *Adam* is in dynamic inter-relationship, not autonomy.

Humanity is then given God's blessing in verse 28. We are not a mere afterthought, brought about because of incessant divine violence. Rather, we are lovingly and graciously created, and then we are blessed and in so many words, told to enjoy the Creator's playground of infinite abundance.

REVELATION TWO: THE PSYCHOLOGY OF HUMANITY'S EXPULSION FROM THE GARDEN (GEN 2:4-3:24)

In the second creation narrative (Gen 2:4–4:26), the story is a bit different.[8] In fact, it is vastly different. It paints a dissimilar picture of God, a God who places prohibitions.[9] But, this dis-similarity is okay, as long as we are able to discern that the goal of this narrative is not like the first. And what is this goal? Well, in my opinion, it is an attempt to elucidate the root causes of violence, which will be forthcoming with the slaughter of Abel at the hands of Cain.

We discussed how prohibitions arise as a culture's attempt to pinpoint what all their fighting was about in the first place. By placing a taboo on something, the community is, in a sense, collectively saying, "That is the *thing* that led to our chaos." In this case, that thing is the "tree of knowledge," or in other words, the desire to have unlimited knowledge, to be just like how we believe God to be. But, when we place prohibitions, our desire becomes "twisted." Remember the red button that we can never push? According to the writer of the second creation story, the tree of the knowledge of good and evil was that red button for not only Eve, but Adam as well—as he was standing next to her the entire time! In fact, it is for all of us as well.

If the tree of the knowledge of good and evil is the red but-ton, then the talking serpent introduced in Gen 3 is the per-verse mimetic desire that pulls us ever-so-hard toward pushing it. Notice how the tale portrays Eve's desire as being enflamed, not within herself, but by another; the serpent. And not only by the serpent, but by the slight twist of the truth the serpent is telling her, which is that God will not let them eat of *any* trees in the gar-den (Gen 3:1). Even in Eve's correction of the serpent, she actu-ally follows the serpent's lead (*mimesis*) and comes up with her own falsification of the details of the first prohibition.[10] Notice how, in accusing God of prohibiting the eating of the fruit of the tree, she ever-so-subtly adds that God will not even allow them to *touch* the tree (Gen 3:3). There is now a rivalry born between Eve and God! By the time the story focuses back on Adam, desire has become so twisted that he imitates Eve in eating of the fruit without as much as a second thought. Then he casts blame upon her as well, also without as much as a second thought (Gen 3:12).

When the two are kicked out of the garden, then, it is not because they broke God's rules, for if it were, then sin would have entered via Eve, not Adam. Rather, they are exiled because of where mimetic rivalry inevitably leads: to violence.

Here's why.

You see, because humans were made to live in partnership, they were made to live in a perfectly egalitarian way with each other and with the Creator. That is the image painted in the first creation narrative, where humankind is given dominion over all of creation. However, in Adam and Eve's "fall," hierarchy is born. And when hierarchy is born, a competition to the top—or, perhaps, to be like God—ensues. When that happens, dominion gives way to domination, which is what we are talking about when we think of "mimetic rivalry." And like we have noticed, this process inevitably leads to violence. The Cain and Abel story from Gen 4, then, will testify to this violence.

REVELATION THREE: THE FOUNDING MURDER RETOLD (GEN 4:1-26)

As we discussed earlier, when introducing a Girardian understanding of mythology, communities tell their stories in such a way that deems the victim guilty of the violence done to them. Founding murder myths assuredly follow this same pattern, as various cultures seem to have similar stories as to how their civilization was founded. As Girard notes, "In Sumerian mythology cultural institutions emerge from a single victim: Ea, Tiamat, Kingu. The same in India: the dismemberment of the primordial victim, Purusha, by a mob offering sacrifices produces the caste system. We find similar myths in Egypt, in China, among the Germanic peoples—everywhere."[11]

In *All Set Free*, I discussed the myth of the founding of the city of Rome. That story tells us how Romulus slays his brother Remus over an omen and is then essentially immortalized with the city being named after him. A similar story is told in the myth of Cadmus, the founder of the Greek city of Thebes. In this tale, after Cadmus slays a dragon, he sows the dragon's teeth into the ground and out rise a group of armed warriors. Immediately, these men begin to slay one another until only five remain. Then they join Cadmus and found Thebes. With this in mind, it is no surprise that when we arrive at the Hebrew version in Gen 4, we find a similar tale (minus the dragon!). However, it will be the differences here that really matter.

The Cain and Abel story begins with an assumption about God; the desire for sacrifice. In fact, this is the very thing that causes the sibling rivalry that will eventually lead to blood. Abel's offering was believed to be favorable in the eyes of God while Cain's was not. To Cain, Abel was now an obstacle for him in achieving such favor and so he murders his brother Abel (Gen 4:8). Now, what is important to notice is that, unlike other murder myths, this story deems Cain guilty of the killing of his brother. It was an unjust slaying and Abel testifies to the truth of that by crying out for blood and vengeance (Gen 4:10). Contrary to other myths, here, the *voice of the victim* is heard. Two things are important to notice about this.

First, in spite of Abel's cry for retribution, God does not consent. In fact, he places a mark on Cain so that nobody would take vengeance, even prophesying that "whoever kills Cain will suffer a sevenfold vengeance" (Gen 4:15). Here, God is not depicted as a retributive deity, but rather, a merciful one. His goal seems to be to stop violence dead in its tracks. The second thing to notice is that Cain senses a credible *outside* threat because of his crime. No doubt, this threat comes from those other than his parents, Adam and Eve. There must be others in the land or I doubt he would say something like, "I shall be a fugitive and a wanderer on the earth, and *anyone* who meets me may kill me" (Gen 4:14—emphasis mine). This is further evidence that we are dealing with a founding murder story, not a literal depiction of the third and fourth human to ever exist.

The next piece of evidence of this rendering comes from the fact that immediately after the murder, a city is founded—Enoch (named after Cain's son). Again, if it were only Cain, his two parents, his wife (where did she come from?), and Cain's son, I hardly think the term "city" is an apt description for Enoch. But city is what it was nonetheless. Romulus had Rome. Cadmus had Thebes. Cain has Enoch, but Cain is no hero of the story. As of yet, there is no hero; only villains. In fact, there are so many villains that after only a few generations, people like Lamech are killing at unprecedented rates. He even boasts, "if Cain is avenged sevenfold, truly Lamech seventy-sevenfold" after murdering a child (Gen 4:24). Man is such that retribution leads to further retribution, a cyclical death spiral in mere generations.

In a very brief time, the human project had gotten desperately out of control. From lies and deception in the garden, to murder as a cultural norm, humankind had pushed the limits of their retribution. Calamity was about to set in, so much so that it would engulf humanity in a flood of epic proportions.

REVELATION FOUR: THE CAUSE OF THE FLOOD (GENESIS 6:5-22)

Like so many accounts of the flood (or deluge, as some cultures called it), the biblical account includes an ark, plenty of animals, and a man whom God was pleased with.[12] The uniqueness in the Hebrew version is what was deemed as the cause to the calamity. Genesis 6:5 tells us that "the wickedness of humankind was great in the earth, and that *every* inclination of the thoughts of their hearts was *only* evil continually" (emphasis mine). Because of this human inclination, *violence* and *corruption* filled the earth (Gen 6:11–13). On three separate occasions, this is emphasized. As Michael Hardin points out: "to be corrupt and full of violence is one and the same thing: this is what scholars call parallelism in Hebrew writing."[13] (The point being driven home is that human violence is what causes the heavens to unleash their fury.)

What began in the garden led to the slaying of Abel, which in six generations led to Lamech killing a boy for a mere scratch, which then led to violence and corruption filling the entire earth—*sans* Noah and his family. Sure, God gets labeled as the sender of the flood but that is because that is the theology at the time. It was frankly *every* culture's theology at the time. Whatever fury nature dealt was only explainable by declaring that "the gods are angry!"

That being said, the Hebrew writer does introduce an understanding of God that is compassionate in spite of being accused of such destruction. Girardian scholar Paul Nuechterlein explains the tension:

> God considered responding to our violence with divine violence and made a promise never to do it again. This perspective on sin looks at all of Gen 3–11 and so views sin as more than just disobedience to God but also, and even primarily, as the forces of rivalrous desire and of violent domination that lead to death. The human enslavement to violence, and the divine commitment to abstain from it, are at odds from the beginning of time.[14]

Now, we will move out of the book of Genesis for a moment and into Exodus, where we will be exploring the Decalogue, or what is commonly known as the Ten Commandments, focusing our attention primarily on commandments 6–10, as they speak directly to the plight humanity finds itself continually in.

REVELATION FIVE: THOU SHALT NOT DESIRE (EXODUS 20:1-17)

The Decalogue is near and dear to countless Jews and Christians alike, as they have been a source of inspiration and strength for millennia. Some even believe that they were a literal dictation directly from God to Moses on Mount Sinai. Regardless as to where one stands on the issue, there should be no denying their profundity. However, as Girard notes at the very beginning of *I See Satan Fall like Lightning*, many fail to discern just *how much* insight can be gained from them, especially in addressing aggression and how desire plays such a large role in it.[15] When read in this light, we will see a compelling correlation to the problem of human violence as testified to in Gen 2–11.

Commandments six through nine are prohibitions that address violence in order from most to least overt. They are as follows:[16]

6. You shall not murder.[17]

7. You shall not commit adultery.

8. You shall not steal.

9. You shall not bear false witness against your neighbor.

Then, the writer really gets to the heart of the issue, the mechanism that leads to violations of the four just-laid-out prohibitions; that of *mimetic desire*. Exodus 20:17 reads: "You shall not covet[18] your neighbor's house; you shall not covet your neighbor's wife, or male or female slave, or ox, or donkey, or anything that belongs to your neighbor." If you will notice, this prohibition is written in quite an interesting way. It is as if the writer was attempting to think of all the things that cause conflict amongst each other before the light bulb goes off: it's the neighbor who is the issue. Our desire is derived from the neighbor. Girard eloquently puts it this way:

> In reading the tenth commandment one has the impression of being present at the intellectual process of its elaboration. To prevent people from fighting, the lawgiver seeks at first to forbid all the objects about which they ceaselessly fight, and he decides to make a list of these. However, he quickly perceives that the objects are too numerous: he cannot enumerate all of them. So he interrupts himself in the process, gives up focusing on the objects that keep changing anyway, and he turns to what never changes. Or rather, he turns to that one who is always present, the neighbor. One always desires whatever belongs to that one, the neighbor.[19]

To see how this may play out in our modern world, perhaps a rewrite of the tenth commandment from a twenty-first century perspective can help.

> Do not desire your neighbor's crib; do not desire your neighbor's spouse, or iPad or PS4, or BMW, or anything that belongs to your neighbor.

If anyone has ventured out on Black Friday or paid attention to the news regarding this now yearly event, then they would no doubt see how desiring what the other has leads to rivalry, aggression, and violence. To avoid these things—and then of paramount importance, those things earlier listed in commandments six through nine—we have to steer clear of entering into mimetic rivalry with others, but most often those closest to us.

While these prohibitions (particularly the tenth) offer great insight into the root cause of violence, the final answer to the problem is not to simply make something taboo. Girard explains: "The disadvantage of the prohibitions, however, is that they don't finally play their role in a satisfying manner. Their primarily negative character, as St. Paul well understood, inevitably provokes in us the mimetic urge to transgress them."[20] In other words, *prohibit something and I just desire it all the more.* That being said, while these prohibitions are not our final answer in solving our problems—in fact, they are our initial answer as our first pillar of culture—they do play a vital role in us eventually arriving at one.

REVELATION SIX: FROM HUMAN TO ANIMAL SACRIFICE (GEN 22:1-18)

As we explored earlier, the practice of sacrifice, in one form or another, is crucial to understanding ritual (the second pillar of culture). What the ritual does is reenact the original violence against the community's scapegoat, while the sacrifice represents the victim himself. Thus, it is a violent system, based on a culture's need to unite together over a corpse. And so, while the Hebrew people indeed engaged in this practice, and might I say heavily so, there is an incremental pull away from this retributive practice of "sacrificing to the gods."

To begin, we will turn to the story of Abraham and Isaac, which is a tough one for most to put their finger on. To be honest, I struggled with it for many years myself.[21] Consider the backdrop for a moment. Here we have a man who does not bear a son with his wife, Sarah, until he is 100 years of age (Gen 21:5). Not exactly the most ideal period in life to procreate! Miraculously though, it happens. A baby boy! But then, one day God decides to "test" Abraham, commanding, "Take your son, your only son[22] Isaac, whom you love,[23] and go to the land of

Moriah, and offer him there as a burnt offering on one of the…"
(Gen 22:2) Wait! What? No, no, no…that cannot be right. It
sounds too ridiculous!

Well, *not so fast*.

If we transport ourselves back in time, perhaps 3,000 years or
more, then we will discover a vastly different culture, with very
specific theological assumptions (starting to sound familiar yet?).
The important thing to understand is that once upon a time, people in the Middle East were polytheists. More specifically, and this
applies to the early Hebrews, they were henotheists.[24] Simply put:
gods were tribal. I had my god, you had your god, and they had
their god. So, for instance, Yahweh was the God of Israel, while
Molech was the god of the Canaanites, and so on and so forth.

With that in mind, let's get back to the story…

What Abraham and Sarah faced religiously and culturally
sounds brutal for any parent. Certainly, they both "knew" that
in order for God to be appeased, blood had to be shed—and
what better blood than that of a first-born son? This was just
the way it was.[25] I believe that is why there is no mention of
Abraham contesting God's "commands." Notice, in Genesis
22:3, immediately after getting the instructions from God, we
are simply told that Abraham "rose early in the morning, saddled
his donkey, and took two of his young men with him, and his
son Isaac." No protesting, no pleading for the boy's life; just that
he saddled up for the journey.

Now, after the two reach the place where Isaac is to be slain,
Abraham immediately builds an altar (Gen 22:9).[26] I can imagine a rudimentary pile of rocks with hefty pieces of wood strate-
gically placed on top. I picture them doused in a flammable oil
of sorts, perhaps something like animal fat. After all, the body
would have to be burned so as to reach the nostrils of God.[27]
Once everything is just right, Abraham binds his beloved Isaac

and takes out his knife. With a shaking hand, he is ready. But all of a sudden, in comes the plot-twist. As Abraham goes to kill Isaac, we read, in Gen 22:11: "But the angel of the Lord called to him from heaven, and said, 'Abraham, Abraham!' And he said, 'Here I am.' He said, 'Do no lay your hand on the boy or do anything to him; for now I know that you fear God, since you have not withheld your son, your only son, from me." Immediately following this, Abraham sees a ram and sacrifices that instead. After he does this, he names the place *Adonai-jireh*, or "The Lord will provide" (Gen 22:14).

In order to determine the power and meaning of this text, we are provided with some very strong clues in the very language used. Notice:

- Verse 1: *Elohim* tested Abraham...

- Verse 3: *Elohim* had shown him...

- Verse 8: *Elohim* himself will provide...

- Verse 9: *Elohim* had shown him...

- Verse 11: But the angel of *Yahweh* called...

Here we have a wrestling with "God's will." Initially, a theological assumption is made about the creator God, Elohim, arguing that he needs Isaac's blood to be spilled. But then the God of Abraham, and then later Isaac, and Jacob, via a messenger angel, rescues Isaac from this false, and might I say murderous, sacrificial assumption. Remember, everyone in Abraham's day believed all gods, Elohim included, demanded blood. But this is simply false. In fact, it is a lie, and ultimately comes from the satan—or in other words, the human principle of accusation—the one whom Jesus would later label a liar and murderer from the start (John 8:44). The lie the satan hides behind here is that God demands blood. The truth, though, is that it is really us as the satan who are the lying, sacrifice-demanding murderers, not *Elohim.*

In all reality, the one true God—whether named Elohim or Yahweh—has never demanded blood sacrifices, but *that* theological understanding is not our starting position; the belief in a God who demands human sacrifice *is.* This passage takes us from one theological place to another. It is a baby step in a way, but it is also huge (especially for me!) because it is ultimately the reason we do not sacrifice first-born sons any longer (and I am a first-born son!).

REVELATION SEVEN: A CRITIQUE OF THE SACRIFICIAL SYSTEM (JER 7:21-23, PS 40:6, HOS 6:6)

"Thus says the Lord of hosts, the God of Israel; Add your burnt offerings to your sacrifices, and eat the flesh. For in the day that I brought your ancestors out of the land of Egypt, I did not speak to them or command them concerning burnt offerings and sacrifices. But this command I gave to them, 'Obey my voice, and I will be your God, and you shall be my people; and walk in the way that I command you, so that it may be well with you.'"

—JER 7:21-23

"Sacrifice and offering you do not desire,
But you have given me an open ear.
Burnt offering and sin offering
You have not required."

—PS 40:6

"For I desire steadfast love and not sacrifice,
The knowledge of God rather than burnt offerings."

—HOS 6:6

In addition to the passages quoted above, there are numerous other anti-sacrificial statements made throughout the Hebrew Scriptures, many of them coming from later prophets.[28] And while we cannot, like any passage, simply read any of them plainly and think matters are *wholly* and *objectively* settled, we can see that within Judaism there is a theological conversation that involves, at the very minimum, a harsh critique of the practice of sacrifice. The above passages are some of the strongest anti-sacrificial statements, contrasting the violent and bloody practice with obeying the voice of God. *I did not do this, but I did that*, says the Lord of hosts. In the passage from Jeremiah specifically, it points to the time when the Israelites were brought out of Egypt, and what they were commanded to do—listen, obey, and walk the path. They were not to create a hierarchal religious system where in which priests make a killing (pardon the pun) while the people remained poor. If sacrifice was to be anything, it was to be a sacrifice of the heart.

If you have the NIV though—the translation that, as of 2013, has more than 450 million copies in print[29]—it will read *just* a bit different, eliminating this contradiction:

> This is what the Lord Almighty, the God of Israel, says: Go ahead, add your burnt offerings to your other sacrifices and eat the meat yourselves! For when I brought your ancestors out of Egypt and spoke to them, I did not *just* give them commands about burnt offerings and sacrifices, but I gave them this command: Obey me, and I will be your God and you will be my people. Walk in obedience to all I command you, that it may go well with you. Jer 7:21–23 NIV

Did you catch that? *Just.* That changes everything, now doesn't it? If God did not *just* give Moses commands regarding sacrifice, then that means he indeed desired blood sacrifices, among other things. But if God did not command the people to sacrifice, then the word "just" needs to be eliminated from our thinking. I believe the latter is true (as the word "just" is not in the Hebrew text) and that the NIV translators, as Michael Hardin so aptly points out "could not handle the possibility that Jeremiah could be in contradiction to Torah and so brought his speech in line with what was in Torah."[30]

That being said, we need to acknowledge that in spite of the critique over the practice of sacrifice, it remained the center of the faith up to and through the life and time of Jesus—until the destruction of the Temple in 70 CE to be precise. So just as the Jewish texts themselves were in travail, so too were the people who read them. Perhaps that is a major reason why Jesus later quotes, on multiple occasions, the "I desire mercy, not sacrifice" passage from Hos 6:6 (Matt 9:13; 12:7). Perhaps it is also the reason the writer of Hebrews has Christ, in Heb 10:6–8, just prior to the incarnation, quoting Ps 40:6–8:

> Sacrifices and offerings you have not desired, but a body you have prepared for me; in burnt offerings and sin offerings you have taken no pleasure. Then I said, "See, God, I have come to do your will, O God" (in the scroll of the book it is written of me)." When he said above, "You have neither desired nor taken pleasure in sacrifices and offerings and burnt offerings and sin offerings" (these are offered according to the law).

In spite of the law requiring blood sacrifices for the forgiveness of sin (Heb 9:22), God neither took pleasure nor desired them (Heb 10:8). Again, sacrifice is contrasted with doing the will of God (Heb 10:7, 9).

Now, for our final three revelations, we will focus our energies on one final concept unique among ancient religions—the voice of the victim. As I mentioned earlier, this uniqueness is introduced when the blood of Cain's victim, Abel, cries out to God from the ground. First, we will be turning back to the book of

Genesis and to the story of Joseph and his brothers. Then, we will explore the book of Job, followed by the poem of the suffering servant from Isa 52—53. And in doing so; we will hopefully pave the way for the introduction of the ultimate victim, Christ Jesus.

REVELATION EIGHT: JOSEPH, THE FORGIVING VICTIM (GEN 37-50)

In chapter 2, we briefly mentioned the myth of King Oedipus. Allow me to summarize that tale again here so that we can then immediately explore the story of Joseph from Gen 37—50. We will do this because of the parallelism between the two stories.

The Oedipus myth begins with the expulsion of a young boy (Oedipus) by his royal family due to an oracle that prophesies he will kill his father (the king of Thebes) and marry his mother (the queen). After Oedipus narrowly escapes with his life, he is then cared for by another king and queen, even being raised as if he was their son. At some point though, he learns of the oracle and, in thinking that his "adoptive" parents are his real parents, flees to Thebes in order to save everyone from the oracle's prediction.

During Oedipus' journey, he quarrels with a stranger and ends up killing him. Unbeknownst to Oedipus, this stranger is really his father, the king of Thebes. When Oedipus learns that the king is deceased and that a Sphinx holds the city captive, he springs into action, solving the riddle and thus freeing Thebes from the Sphinx's grasp. As a reward, Oedipus received—you guessed it!—the throne, thus fulfilling the prophecy. When Oedipus later learns of this fulfillment, it is said that Apollo sends a great plague on Thebes so that the people would expel their king from the city. When they do, the plague is lifted and peace returns.

Now, when we turn to the story of Joseph, we will notice striking similarities. But we will also notice striking dissimilarities as well, which are crucial for our attention.

Like the Oedipus myth, the story of Joseph starts out with a vision (Gen 37:1–11). In this tale though, the visions come in the form of dreams, which all point to the fact that, sometime in the future, one day all of his brothers would bow down and serve Joseph. This infuriates the brothers so they plot to kill him (just like Oedipus' parents did when they learned of the oracle). But, like Oedipus, Joseph narrowly escapes (Gen 37:21).

Then, he is sold into slavery (Gen 37:25–28), deceived by an Egyptian woman (Potiphar's wife), and imprisoned under false pretenses (Gen 39:1–20). But, because he has the gift of interpreting dreams, Joseph quickly garners the attention and even affection of the Pharaoh, until one day, Joseph is made Vizier, that is, Pharaoh's right hand man (Gen 41:37–57). At this point, it is fascinating to see how both tales—that of Oedipus and also this one—attribute the main character's ability to solve/interpret riddles as what leads to their rise in status. For Oedipus, he is made king of Thebes because he solved the riddle of the Sphinx. For Joseph, he rises to power because of his ability to solve the riddle of the Pharaoh's dreams (which predicted how the land would experience seven years of abundance followed by seven years of famine).

Now, during the time of the famine, Joseph's brothers travel to Egypt to purchase much needed grain. Long story short: after Joseph deceives the brothers with what seemed like an ill-thought-out plan, he ends the charades and reveals his identity (Gen 45:3). But he does not do so with anger or malice in his heart, but instead, with mercy. Gen 45:4–5 reads: "Then Joseph said to his brothers, 'Come closer to me.' And they came closer. He said, 'I am your brother, Joseph, whom you sold into Egypt.

And now do not be distressed, or angry with yourselves, because you sold me here; for God sent me before you to preserve life."

Finally, after their father, Jacob, passes away, the story concludes with Joseph ultimately forgiving his brothers (who feared retribution) for their original treachery, which then causes all of them to fall at Joseph's feet (Gen 50:15–21). Thus, the original dream that they would serve him was fulfilled.

Indeed, the moral of the Joseph story is the opposite of myth (the third pillar of culture)! Remember, the city of Thebes finds deliverance from the curse *after* they expel a guilty Oedipus. The king did the crime, and so he had to be sent away. But the Joseph story states the opposite. Joseph is not guilty of anything, the brothers are. In spite of that though, the victim offers forgiveness. This is what then brings reconciliation.

REVELATION NINE: JOB THE SCAPEGOAT (JOB 1-42)

The book of Job poetically presents just how easily we scapegoat even our supposed "friends," showing how the suffering of those at which the community points their collective fingers of condemnation. It is for that reason that Michael Hardin correctly calls it "an extended psalm of lament."[31] If you read through the book yourself, you will unmistakably see how the themes of scapegoating and lamentation, as told by the voice of the victim, are indeed front and center.

The book of Job begins with a dialogue between God and the satan.[32] Many view this conversation, where God entices the satan to test Job (Job 1:8), as the interpretive lens from which to read the rest of the book.[33] But, as Hardin writes: "the Dialogues (Job 3–37) present us with the 'truth' that is papered over in the dualism of the Prologue. The victimization of Job by his community is turned into a heavenly prosecution."[34] That is to say, the

scene between God and the satan is there to justify the friends'
scapegoating of Job, to make Job's plight out to be divinely man-
dated. Let us get into the specifics of that now.

After we read about how Job suffers great tragedy—property,
children, and then health—his friends arrive to "console and
comfort him" (Job 2:11). But quickly, their comforting turns to
accusations—in the name of God of course. Of the friends and
their theology, Girard writes: "The theology of the four friends is
nothing but an expression...of the theology of violence and the
sacred. Any sufferer could not suffer except for a good reason in
a universe governed by divine justice."[35] That is to say, a universe
governed by divine retributive justice, which we have discovered
to be an anthropological projection.

So, with that in mind, the first friend, Eliphaz, offers the
following "advice": "Think now, who that was innocent ever
perished? Or where were the upright cut off? As I have seen,
those who plow iniquity and sow trouble reap the same" (Job
4:7–8). In short: Job was reaping what he had sown; iniquity
begetting iniquity. Bildad's "guidance" is no better. "See, God
will not reject a blameless person, nor take the hand of evildo-
ers" (Job 8:20). Lastly, Zophar implies that Job's wickedness is
the cause of his suffering when he states, "If iniquity is in your
hand, put it far away, and do not let wickedness reside in your
tents" (Job 11:14–15). Yet things get even more inflammatory.
Eliphaz later accuses Job of very specific crimes: "For you have
exacted pledges from your family for no reason, and stripped the
naked of their clothing. You have given no water to the weary to
drink, and you have withheld bread from the hungry...You have
sent widows away empty-handed, and the arms of the orphans
you have crushed" (Job 22:6–7, 9). So, what is Job's response?
And are the accusations fair? Or, is this gossiping all a part of the
scapegoating process?

Well, according to Job, it was not fair. Job's first retort is that his complaints are just (Job 6:1). He is even willing to "be silent" so that he can understand where he went wrong (Job 6:24). So, unlike the implications of Job's "friends," he *was* willing to change. My friend and colleague Adam Ericksen explains: "In the face of satanic accusations levied against him, Job maintains his innocence. He does not claim to be sinless, but does contend that he does not deserve the suffering inflicted upon him."[36] Job's theology, however, like that of his "friends," indeed mandates that his sufferings were his fault. But no answer as to why he had to suffer comes from above—nothing concrete and truthful, just more and more accusations from the community.

The wicked truth about human community, as testified to in the book of Job, is only cemented then in the lamenting of the main character. Job speaks most honestly about the plight of the scapegoat, the one everyone shames, ridicules, and excommunicates. Seemingly, the entire planet is against him. Even his inanimate clothes abhor him (Job 9:31). And, as Ericksen stated, Job accurately calls it like it is: he is not guilty of what he is being accused of.[37] In terms of wickedness and iniquity, he is no worse than those around him, and not guilty of the supposed divine punishment or the sufferings further amplified by the scapegoating community.

This leads us to yet another reality the book of Job speaks to: the retributive God model does not work. It puts us in a place where we look to the life situations of those around us to deem whether they are under "God's blessing" or "God's curse." And then for scriptural support, we will turn to places like Deut 28:15, 20–24, and 58–61. But because of Job, the victim of his people, this ethical dilemma that stems from a retributive theological framework is exposed as rubbish. People end up looking like Job's friends, who, in the name of God actually become the *satan*, the accusers of others.

At the end of Job's story though, after all of the suffering he had endured, his fortunes are restored (Job 42:10). Prior to his death, he accumulates great wealth and his daughters are said to be the most beautiful in the land (Job 42:15). But the way in which things work out for Job, especially from a theological standpoint, leaves a lot to be desired. Not only does his ending fail to address the problem of a retributive theology, but it also fails to address the ethical concerns this theology can lead to. Moreover, it paints God as a God with, as Michael Hardin calls it, a "macho attitude."[38] On a few occasions, God tells Job to "gird up your loins like a man" (Job 38:3; 40:7). It is as if God is saying, "Hey, sorry that I had the *satan* come trash your life by killing your children and giving you boils, but be a man for goodness' sake!" Then God goes through all the ways in which he is bigger, better, and "badder" than Job.

But all of this is okay for us today, because the revelatory truth contained in the book is found in the dialogues (Job 3–37), namely with the voice of the victim, not in the voices of the accusatory characters. Their voices are exposed as satanic by the one who cries out for a God who can come to the defense of a victim. And although defense comes in an unsatisfactory way, it does come. God is not on the side of the accusers, but on the side of the victims. Or, as God tells the friends in Job 42:8, "You have not spoken of me what is right, as my servant Job has done."

Now, finally we turn to Isa 52—53, the poem of the suffering servant. It is tragic, in my opinion, that many Christians have used this poem to argue for a penal substitutionary atonement theory, in which God uses the suffering servant to pour out his wrath upon. In reality, however, this notion would be a complete anomaly for the Hebrew Scriptures, a "one of a kind" thing.[39]

And, although it is quite popular in certain theological streams, will we see how it may not be the best interpretation of what is really going on here.

REVELATION TEN: THE SUFFERING SERVANT (ISAIAH 52:13-53:12)

Like Job, the suffering servant of Isaiah is a human scapegoat. However, it should also be seen as a poem "related to known historical facts."[40] That is to say, we should look at the passages at hand as presenting the nation of Israel as a suffering servant of Yahweh.[41] However, and more importantly for our purposes, we should also notice how Jesus can easily be read back into this poem as he certainly fits the description. But we will get to that in due time. First though, we need to explore the opening declaration from God.

In Isa 52:13–15, the divine voice dramatically begins:

See, my servant will act wisely;
he will be raised and lifted up and highly exalted.
Just as there were many who were appalled at him—
his appearance was so disfigured beyond that of any human being
and his form marred beyond human likeness—
So he will sprinkle many nations,
and kings will shut their mouths because of him.
For what they were not told, they will see,
and what they have not heard, they will understand.

What God is said to be describing regarding the horror that befalls his servant is antithetical to how God created us (Gen 1:26–27). Anthony Bartlett observes the connection this way: "The picture is a contradiction of Genesis where man and woman are made in the image of God; it is both a human and a theological reversal, an absolute dehumanization."[42] It is also God's way of redefining power.[43] Rather than kings shutting their mouths due to being overwhelmed by the military might of the enemy, they will shut them by a humble servant "so disfigured beyond that of any human being" (Isa 52:14).

In contrast to the divine voice in 52:13–15, chapter 53 starts off collectively.

> For he grew up before him like a young plant,
> and like a root out of dry ground;
> He had no form or majesty that we should look at him,
> nothing in his appearance that we should desire him.
> He was despised and rejected by others;
> a man of suffering and acquainted with infirmity;
> And as one from whom others hide their faces
> he was despised, and we held him of no account. (Isa 53:2–3)

As we have discovered, scapegoats are often those who stand out amongst the other community members—those despised, those who are sick, those whose roots grow out of dry ground, one could say. Their purpose, then, is to bear the violence of the community so as to become the bringer of peace. And as I have stated on numerous occasions, all of this is, in the minds of the mob, "divinely ordained." This is why 53:4–10a read as follows:

> Surely he has borne our infirmities
> and carried our diseases;
> Yet we accounted him stricken,
> struck down by God, and afflicted.
> But he was wounded for our transgressions,
> crushed for our iniquities;
> Upon him was the punishment that made us whole,
> and by his bruises we are healed.
> All we like sheep have gone astray;
> we have all turned to our own way,
> and the Lord has laid on him
> the iniquity of us all.
> He was oppressed, and he was afflicted,
> yet he did not open his mouth;
> like a lamb that is led to the slaughter,

and like a sheep that before its shearers is silent,
so he did not open his mouth.
By a perversion of justice he was taken away.
Who could have imagined his future?
For he was cut off from the land of the living,
stricken for the transgression of my people.[44]
They made his grave with the wicked
and his tomb with the rich,
although he had done no violence,
and there was no deceit in his mouth.
Yet it was the will of the Lord to crush him with pain.

Certainly, this looks like a divinely-ordained lynching. Notice how the collective voice puts their actions so obviously in the category of "God's will" by attaching "we" to "God/the Lord."

- Verse 4: *We* accounted him stricken...

- Verse 4: Struck down by *God*, and afflicted.

- Verse 6: *The Lord* has laid on him the iniquity of us all.

- Verse 10: It was the will of *the Lord* to crush him...

Over and over, we have seen the perspective that the violence the community pours onto the random scapegoated victim is believed to be divine in origin. *It is the will of the gods.* Verses 4–10 are no different.

But God clarifies what his righteous will is in his response in vv 11–12, most specifically in 11a. They read:

Out of his anguish he shall see light;
he shall find satisfaction through his knowledge.
The righteous one, my servant, shall make many righteous,
and he shall bear their iniquities.
Therefore I will allot him a portion with the great,
and he shall divide the spoil with the strong;
because he poured out[45] himself to death,
and was numbered with the transgressors;
yet he bore the sin of many,
and made intercession for the transgressors.

What is being said here is that the servant willingly gives up his life (*nefesh*), non-violently (Isa 53:9), for the very people who put him to death. He sees the profundity of what he is suffering through and so, gains an understanding and a knowledge that makes "many" righteous (Isa 53:11). The knowledge that the servant earns is a recognition of both God's desires and of what it means to be human. Bartlett calls it a "new theological-anthropological truth."[46] To be righteous—that is to say, to be like God—is to be like the suffering servant, the one who has no violence in him (Isa 53:9). James G. Williams drives this point further home with the following: "It wasn't God who caused his suffering, it was oppressors. As the divine voice says in an oracle found in chapter 54: 'If any one stirs up strife, it is not from me; whoever stirs up strife with you shall fall because of you.' (Isa 54:15) 'Strife'—the conflict of mimetic rivalry that results in violence—does not come from God."[47]

FROM THE OLD TO THE NEW…TESTAMENT, THAT IS

We have now come to the end of our journey through the Hebrew Scriptures. What we have focused our attention on is the growing and changing understanding of God, often away from violence and toward mercy and peace. That is to say, there is progressive revelation taking place throughout the Hebrew Scriptures. We see this in the story of Cain and Abel, in Abraham and Isaac, in many of the psalms and in the writings of the later prophets, and elsewhere.

In addition to our progressing theological understanding, the Hebrew Scriptures also give us profound insights into what humans are like. In the second creation narrative from Genesis, as well as in the second half of the Decalogue, we have an amazing look into the human psyche, specifically with regards to desire and the consequences of it. In the book of Job, we see just how cruel the scapegoating mechanism can be. We bear witness to the fact that even our friends, who are often just there to help and give comfort; can also become our most rigid accusers—in the name of their (retributive) theology of course. This violent scapegoating mechanism is also at play in the story of Joseph and his brothers and in the suffering servant of Isaiah, as I just mentioned in the previous section. It is portrayed as so vicious in fact, that God's own servant becomes void of "human semblance" (Isa 52:14)—a dehumanization of the highest degree!

With this in mind, we will now take a look at the life of Jesus of Nazareth. But to understand his message and the death and resurrection, we need to make sure we have a basic comprehension of the appropriate religious, cultural, and political context of Jesus' day. Sadly, per my experience, many do not do this. Instead, what they seem to do is pluck Jesus from the first-century and drop him anywhere from the sixteenth to the twenty-first century. What results is a grossly distorted view of his teachings and lessons, his hermeneutics, as well as his actions and ethics. To the contrary, our goal will be to bear his culture in mind, so as to not paint a picture of Jesus that never really existed. Understanding an appropriate context will be crucial if we are going to then discern all the many ways in which he offers humanity a completely new "theological-anthropological truth," as Bartlett calls it.[48]

CHAPTER 5

THE GOSPEL OF CHRIST JESUS: AN APOCALYPSE OF GOD AND OF THE TRUE HUMAN

"Thus in this oneness Jesus Christ is the Mediator, the Reconciler, between God and man. He comes forward to man on behalf of God calling for and awakening faith, love, and hope, and to God on behalf of man, representing man, making satisfaction and interceding. Thus he attests and guarantees to man God's free grace and at the same time attests and guarantees to God man's free gratitude."[1]

–KARL BARTH

FRAMING AN APPROPRIATE FIRST-CENTURY JEWISH CONTEXT

First and foremost, Jesus was Jewish. I know, shocking, right? More specifically though, he was a Jew who lived in what is known as the Second Temple period.[2] During this time, there were multiple sects and various different ways to approach the faith. Michael Hardin calls it a "multi-flowered" Judaism.[3] Part of the "multi-flowered" nature of the faith was the various approaches to Torah. The Pharisees for instance, were sort of the "liberals" of the day (when compared to the Sadducees). They contended that, in addition to the written law of Torah, oral law was given by God to Moses as well. The Sadducees flat-out rejected such a claim. For them, the Law was in written form only. A third group, the Essenes, who arose because of a disdain for both the Pharisees and Sadducees, essentially believed all of Torah, oral and written, needed to be exegeted by "inspiration." So, who was correct? The Pharisees? The Sadducees? The Essenes? Yet others?[4]

Competition for "correct doctrine," as well as political control, led to tension and strife. The Sadducees were, as Vincent Gabriel puts it, "the party most favorable to the secular rulers."[5] It is no wonder, then, why historian Lester Grabbe comically says of them: "The Sadducees have been everyone's whipping boy. No Jewish group today claims to be heirs of the Sadducees."[6] (Indeed, nobody likes being associated with corrupt politics.) They were countered by the Pharisees, who saw the Sadducees as "compromised."[7] For the Pharisees, zeal for the law was paramount. Thus, they were to be ritualistically "pure," set apart from the "unclean" Gentiles (and those who would associate with them). The Essenes shared these sentiments with the Pharisees and would go so far as to live a life in the wilderness, away from the Temple and mainstream Jewish religious and cultural life.[8]

In addition to the theological and political tension between these factions, there was friction in the streets due to the poor living standards of much of the population. The gap between the haves and the have nots was huge. The fact that many of the haves were the also the leaders of the faith did not help things. Many of the sick and poor were pushed to the margins of society by the ruling class, scapegoated for their "iniquities." And again, the belief in a retributive God, where blessing is bestowed upon the "righteous" (those in charge) and wrath on the "wicked" (the poor and afflicted), had very real consequences on society.

Lastly, Jews in the Second Temple period were ruled by arguably the most brutal empire the world has ever known. Living in a Roman-occupied province meant that Jesus had to obey Roman law, which was often enforced by the business end of a spear. This was especially true any time anyone posed a threat to their version of peace, or *Pax Romana*, as it was known. Some of the various Jewish understandings of messiahship would be viewed by Rome as such a threat, as it was often associated with violence and revolution.[9] It had to be, for how else were the Jews going to be delivered from such a beast as Rome? Jewish Jubilee rested on the hopes that the messiah would violently overthrow their oppressors (see Isa 61:1–2). Figures like Simon of Peraea (ca. 4 BCE) and Athronges (ca. 4-2 BCE) both fit the description of a "violent messiah-type revolutionary." So, because Jesus eventually became associated with the term "messiah," as well as for a variety of other reasons, he will often find himself in the crosshairs of violence.

Keeping this theological and political setting in the back of our minds, we now turn to Jesus and to the journey which he called his followers to embark on. We begin with Jesus' first lesson after his baptism and subsequent calling into the wilderness by the Holy Spirit (Luke 4:1–13). This will be the first thing a Spirit-filled Jesus teaches after conquering his dark side.[10] That is why I believe it is a good place to begin this part of our journey.

JESUS' HERMENEUTICS

A SABBATH TO REMEMBER

Imagine that you are living in first-century Nazareth. You are at the synagogue on a fine Sabbath afternoon when Jesus walks in.

Nobody that you know has seen him since his baptism in the Jordan. Forty days and nothing! But here he comes now. You think to yourself: *Where has he been? What has he been doing?* You look around and conclude that each person must have been thinking this same thing because everyone has that look of anticipation on their face.

After a time, it becomes Jesus' turn to read. He stands up, and the attendant of the synagogue walks over and hands him the scroll of the prophet Isaiah. Without hesitation, Jesus searches for a passage. You notice that he seems to know exactly where he is going. But before you can even predict which passage, Jesus stops.

He takes a brief pause, gathers himself, and reads:

"The Spirit of the Lord is upon me,
　　because he has anointed me
　　　　to bring good news to the poor.
He has sent me to proclaim release to the captives
　　and recovery of sight to the blind,
　　　　to let the oppressed go free,
to proclaim the year of the Lord's favor." (Luke 4:18–19)

Then Jesus rolls up the scroll and gives it back to the attendant.

Befuddled you think: *Hasn't he forgotten something from this Jubilee passage?* Surely, Jesus is aware that Isaiah 61:2 reads: "to proclaim the year of the Lord's favor, *and the day of vengeance of our God*" (emphasis mine). But no, he does not seem to think he has forgotten anything. Jesus concludes: "Today this scripture has been fulfilled in your hearing" (Luke 4:21).

At this point, things begin to get contentious.[11] One member of the crowd even sarcastically retorts, "Is not this Joseph's son?" (Luke 4:22) But Jesus is having none of it! He counters: "Truly I tell you, no prophet is accepted in the prophet's hometown. But the truth is, there were many widows in Israel in the time of Elijah, when the heaven was shut up three years and six months, and there was a severe famine over all the land; yet Elijah was sent to none of them except to a widow at Zarephath in Sidon.

There were also many lepers in Israel in the time of the prophet Elisha, and none of them were cleansed except Naaman the Syrian" (Luke 4:24–27).

Now things start to explode. You are at your wits end. Not only does Jesus come in here with his "creative interpretation" of Isaiah, but then he has the nerve to go on about how Israel's prophets aided and comforted outsiders, heathens, hated-people of God. Does Jesus even realize that Naaman was a warrior pitted against the chosen people of God?[12] Thoughts are racing through your head: *How can Israel be delivered if God isn't vengeful? How can a prophet suggest God has such care for our enemies, the Sidonites and the Syrians? Who does Jesus think he is! Some prophet!*

You are not alone in your rage. Everyone is starting to become irate and in doing so, begin to validate each other's anger. Jesus takes quick action and backs away as you and the others close in on him. Driving this fool from the synagogue, he is forced out of town toward the edge of a nearby cliff. Now's your chance! You go to reach for him but he slips from your grasp. In fact, somehow, he slips past everyone. Furious, you shove your way through the crowd and head back to the synagogue, where you are convinced blasphemy had just taken place in a most overt way.

Okay, so I realize that we took creative liberty on some of the details of the story. But the truth of it remained. What I wanted to do was paint a picture of the anticipation people would have likely had prior to Jesus' first (recorded[13]) post-baptism teaching, to envision the disappointment they would have felt after having heard such a "creative" reading of such a popular passage from Isaiah.[14] Moreover, I wanted us to taste the rage they would have felt if some "prophet" came into their synagogue to challenge their theology and to strip them of the only thing they had over and against the Romans; namely divine retribution.[15]

Jesus is going to do something similar when addressing some of John the Baptist's disciples. In fact, for this next story, we will be stepping into John the Baptist's sandals, in order to "experience" what Jesus is creatively, yet consistently, pursuing.

GO AND TELL JOHN

It has been some time since King Herod has imprisoned you (Luke 3:20). You just couldn't help but speak out against the Herodian family system and Herod had had enough.[16] From your jail cell you wonder whether Jesus is "the one who is to come" that you have spoken about (Luke 3:16–17). You are perplexed because Jesus just did not *quite* fit the description you and most all others had in mind. To be honest, many are still stuck in the mindset that *vengeance* can be found in the divine.[17] You've even said as much (Luke 3:7–9). But there was *something* about Jesus and you have to find out the truth. So you send some of your disciples to Jesus in order to ask him the burning questions that you need answered.

When your disciples find Jesus, they ask him if he is the one. Instead of a straight forward "yes" or "no" answer, he offers the following: "Go and tell John what you have seen and heard: the blind receive their sight, the lame walk, the lepers are cleansed, the deaf hear, the dead are raised, the poor have good news brought to them. And blessed is anyone who takes no offense at me" (Luke 7:22–23). But you know this about Jesus already. You are aware of the miracles. Isn't that a part of why you would be sending your disciples to Jesus in the first place? So what is Jesus *really* saying?

You start to think. As you reflect, you fix your mind on the Scriptures. You list everything Jesus says happens on account of him:

- *The blind receive their sight* (from Isa 29:18; 35:5; 61:1–2)

- *The lame walk* (from Isa 35:6)

- *The lepers are cleansed* (from 2 Kgs 5:1–27)

- *The deaf hear* (from Isa 29:18; 35:5)

- *The dead are raised* (from 1 Kgs 17:17–24)

- *The poor have good news brought to them* (from Isa 29:19)

After pondering for some time on what Jesus could possibly be doing here, it dawns on you. Every quote from Isaiah that Jesus makes has an attached phrase that invokes the "vengeance of God" that you yourself hold on to. By leaving that part off, Jesus is giving you clues into his mission and the nature of God. Isa 29:20: "~~And those alert to do evil shall be cut off.~~" Isa 35:4: "~~Here is your God. He will come with vengeance.~~" And Isa 61:2: "~~And the day of vengeance of our God.~~"

Then the clincher comes, when Jesus says: "And blessed is anyone who takes no offense at me" (Luke 7:23). Surely, this offense that he is causing is the same one he caused in the people at the synagogue in Nazareth (Luke 4:18–30). This is the offense of a non-retributive God. This is the scandal caused by a God who blesses both the righteous and the wicked (Matt 5:45). This is the problem almost all seem to have when others suggest divinity transcends borders—*religious* and *national*—in order to bless everyone. But Jesus wants you to take comfort and be blessed by not taking offense at this reality, this divine truth.

Now, I have no idea whether John the Baptist ever accepted Jesus as "the one who is to come." Perhaps Herod executed John without him ever really knowing the truth. My point then was to simply model what Jesus was doing when he creatively answers John's disciples. Like his creative reading of Isa 61:1–2 (from Luke 4:18–19), Jesus is offering clues into how he views his heavenly Father. And he offers insight into the fruit that one reaps when they can accept this non-vengeful understanding of God…"Blessed is anyone who takes no offense at me."

Now let's head on over to Matt 5, where Jesus will offer what is undoubtedly one of the most radical teachings in all of the New Testament. It is also a place where Jesus continues his creative interpretation of the Jewish Scriptures, consistently framing a new picture of both God and of the human being.

YOU HAVE HEARD THAT IT WAS SAID

There is a buzz in the air. You have caught word of a man named Jesus, who has been "proclaiming the good news of the kingdom and curing every disease and every sickness among the people" (Matt 4:23). No doubt, you have heard, even seen *some things* in your life, but there is something different about this man. So you go to the mountain where he—just like Moses thousands of years prior—is preaching, in hopes of listening in.

Immediately, you are drawn to his teachings. They resonate deep within you and so you cannot help but be intrigued. *Blessed are the poor in spirit, those who mourn, the meek, those who hunger and thirst for righteousness, the merciful, and the pure in heart, the peacemakers, and those who are persecuted for righteousness' sake* (Matt 5:3–10). But Jesus doesn't stop there. He goes on, offering profound teaching after profound teaching concerning such things as anger, adultery, divorce, making oaths, retaliation, and enemy love. You think to yourself: *Yes! What amazing things this man is saying. This is what we've been waiting for!*

Amidst your excitement, you also notice something interesting: which is, that Jesus is using a certain tactic in his teaching. You see, over the years, you have become quite adept at memorizing large portions of the Scriptures. So you take note, that on multiple occasions, Jesus begins a teaching from Torah, and then follows that by putting a unique interpretive "spin" on it. The parts you really gravitate toward are his commands on radical nonviolence. You smile to yourself as you bear witness to this teacher boldly preaching to disavow the "eye for an eye" mindset (Matt 5:38–42), even though many of your interlocutors argue that the Scriptures *clearly state* justice is defined as such in Lev 24:19–21. You hear him teach to love thine enemy (Matt 5:44), even though many of your religious brothers and sisters, following in the footsteps of many of your forefathers, assuredly refused to do so. And you hear this Jesus teach of a God who sends rain on the righteous and on the unrighteous (Matt 5:45), even though this is a direct contradiction of what most have taught, which is that God's "curse is on the house of the wicked" (Prov 3:33).

After Jesus concludes his teachings, you head home blessed and inspired. The more he spoke, the more his words resonated with you. They were parabolic, full of mystery and intrigue, and contained enough depth to keep any seeker of God busy their entire life. You can't help but think: *What kind of prophet is this?* A part of you even believes that he could be "the one," but it is far too early to tell. Besides, predictions aren't your thing anyway. Not only that, but what Jesus was teaching was not exactly normal for most messianic expectations.[18] Yet, you knew that this man was something to behold and that people should probably pay attention to him regardless. Your only fear then, based on how radical he seemed, is that *certain* people eventually would.[19]

As you can probably tell, my purpose in highlighting what I did, was to elucidate the continuity in how Jesus exegetes the Hebrew Scriptures. In Luke 4 and 7, Jesus omits any portion of a passage that mentions the alleged "vengeance of God." He will even stop a quote midsentence if he has to, as he does when he quotes Isa 61:2. And then in Matt 5, Jesus changes our entire thinking about God when he argues that the perfection of the Heavenly Father is defined by a love for enemies and a blessing of both the wicked and the righteous.[20]

I contend that all of this reframing is done because many Jews in the Second Temple period had certain retributive theological expectations. That is to say, they believed that God blesses Israel (that is, when they are obeying God) and punishes those who disobey (that is, their enemies or the powers that control them politically). In most people's minds, "God is for 'us' and against 'them.'" But, in stark contrast, highlighted in Matt 5, Jesus announces that God is for us and that there is no "them!"

THE GREATEST COMMANDMENT

If you think back to chapter 4, you should recall our discussion of how the prohibitions found in the Decalogue (primarily the tenth commandment) address a fundamental human problem, that of mimetic desire, without offering a way to address said desire. That is to say while the prohibiting of what belongs to our neighbor is a valiant attempt at stopping rivalry and violence, it doesn't actually solve anything as prohibited items always drive us to desire them even more. It is that whole "red button" problem again. That being said, we are now at the place in our journey where, because of Jesus, we can gain insights into an appropriate interpretation of the Decalogue—nay, the whole of the law and prophets—one that, if applied, can actually offer a way to truly eliminate rivalry and violence.

Turning to Matt 22:34–40, we will now explore exactly how Jesus lays out this hermeneutical approach to all of the law and prophets, summing up the entire law (Torah) and the prophets with two overarching commands. And not only are they the sum of all the law and prophets, but they are interrelated—two sides of the same coin, if you will (Matt 22:39). In other words, you really cannot do one without the other. The commandments are as follows: "You shall love the Lord your God with all your heart, and with all your soul, and with all your mind" (Matt 22:37); and: "You shall love your neighbor as yourself" (Matt 22:39). What should be noticed is that, unlike the first and tenth commandment from the Decalogue (Exod 20 and Deut 5), which both focus on a prohibition—"you shall have *no* other gods before me," and "you shall *not* desire anything that belongs to your neighbor"—Jesus commands, not a prohibition, but rather, an action. You *shall* love God and you *shall* love your neighbor as yourself.

As we explored in chapter 2, prohibitions just don't cut it. In fact, because they twist our desire, it can be argued that they make it worse.[21] And Jesus knows this. So, as Girard puts it, "he draws out the full consequences of the lesson offered by the tenth commandment."[22] That is to say, Jesus takes the goal of the prohibitions, which is peace, and turns them into a command about love, which will be the key to achieving peace. But this raises the question "How does one 'Love God and neighbor?'" And a valid follow-up question is "Who, exactly, is my neighbor?" First, we will answer the latter question. Then, we will use the remainder of this chapter to answer the former.

In the Lukan narrative of the greatest commandment, Jesus, in typical Jesus fashion, answers who our neighbor is with a parable (Luke 10:25–37). He tells of a man who is beaten by a group of robbers. Left for dead on the side of the road, this man is visited by three different people. First, a priest sees the dying man but does not help. Instead, he passes by on the opposite side of the road. The second, a Levite, does the very same thing. It is not until a Samaritan walks by that the dying man receives treatment. Not only does the Samaritan bandage the man's wounds, but he also brings him to an inn and takes care of him.

So what is Jesus *really* saying? Michael Hardin makes the analogy: "It would be like saying a TV preacher and a priest walked by a wounded Christian, but an Islamic terrorist stopped to aid him. This parable has shock value, or it should."[23] This shock value should be present due to the fact that the Samaritan is the so-called "enemy" of the Jews. Like the Sidonite and Syrian from Luke 4, they are not supposed to be the heroes of the story! But as Jesus often does, he flips perceptions on their head. Here, he is teaching that who our religion and culture defines as "the enemy other" is actually supposed to be emulated. That is to say, the neighborly thing for them to do is to always treat "enemies" with mercy, just like the Samaritan did for the dying man in the parable (Luke 10:37).

So, if we refer back to the two questions posed earlier, Jesus moves us past the first question, of who our neighbor is, to the second—and more important—question, namely *how* one is to love our neighbor. But this one lesson is just the tip of the iceberg. Jesus will continue to be teacher and guide in this, and to put it in Girardian terms, be the model of positive mimesis that we are to imitate in order to avoid the mimetic rivalries we are so prone to. Jesus offers himself as a living, and breathing model for us to follow and thus imitate. And what that model will primarily be focused on is the forgiveness and reconciliation of those whom others have then banished and cursed. Thus, this will be our answer to "how do we love God and neighbor?"

In order to explore this model better, we will once again employ an imaginative reading of a couple of passages that carry with them the theme of forgiveness and reconciliation. The first place we will travel to is John 8—to the temple—to witness Jesus through the eyes of an adulterous woman condemned to death by her people. Remember, this is an imaginative reading, so some of the details have been added for dramatic effect.

JESUS' LIFE AND MISSION

HAS ANYONE CONDEMNED YOU?

You have been married for three years, but the past two have been spent in a state of despair. Sure, the first few months were filled with passion, but that fire quickly burned out and love grew cold. In your weakness, you made the choice to step outside of your marriage commitment and find "love" in the arms of another man. But this lapse in judgment would nearly be your undoing when your husband—and then what must have seemed like the rest of the city—discovered your lust-filled romp.

After you are seized for your crime, the scribes and Pharisees take you to the temple. They bring you to a man named Jesus, who was teaching a group who had come to listen to him. The Pharisees ask him "Teacher, this woman was caught in the very act of committing adultery. Now in the law Moses commanded us to stone such women. Now what do you say?" (John 8:4–5) Instantly, your heart starts racing faster and faster. You quiver with fright and anticipation as this unknown teacher seems to hold your fate in his hands.

Jesus doesn't answer immediately. He stoops down and begins to write in the sand. *What is he doing?* you ponder. Finally, after further questioning from the scribes, Jesus replies: "Let anyone among you who is without sin be the first to throw a stone at her" (John 8:7). Immediately, a silence falls over the place. You glance over at one of your accusers only to see a look of puzzle across his face. You turn to your right and see the same stupefied look on two of the Pharisees. Then, one by one, they start to leave. The scribe who was closest to you can only shake his head and mutter something unrecognizable as he walks by.

Finally, it is just you and Jesus. You feel relieved that the "authorities" dispersed, but remain anxious about what this teacher might say to you. After a moment, he stands up and rhetorically asks: "Woman, where are they? Has no one condemned you?" (John 8:10) With a quivering chin and a barely-audible voice, you muster an answer: "No one, sir" (John 8:11). Tears now start flowing down your cheeks. Compassionately, Jesus offers you one final word: "Neither do I condemn you. Go your way, and from now on do not sin again" (John 8:11).

What Jesus does here is simply amazing. He, being the only one without sin and thus the only one present that would have the moral authority to condemn the adulterous woman, chooses to offer mercy, which in turn gives her the ability to be potentially reconciled back into right relationship with her husband, as well as the community. In short: mercy triumphs even when punishment is "just," even when the Scriptures are *clearly* on the side of the accusatory Pharisees. Yet, not only does Jesus offer this radical mercy, but he also does so by then turning the Pharisaical "interpretation"—or rather, proof-texting—of Torah against the Pharisees themselves. When he does this, he strips those who are looking for victims of their power over others. Michael Hardin explains:

> A violent interpretation of Torah is also the issue in the story of the woman taken in adultery in John 7:53—8:11. There the Pharisees and scribes seek to trap Jesus into acknowledging that the Torah justifies social violence…Jesus can either affirm the validity of the commandment or he can deny it. He does neither. What he does it [sic] to point out that the one who cannot be judged by the Law has the right to throw the first stone. As each one looked to his life, they realized that at some point large or small, neither had they kept the commandments. So, they dropped their stones.[24]

In our next imaginative reading, we will be turning to Jesus' healing of a blind man. In this story, we will be examining two things. First, we will pay attention to the theology of the characters of the story, which posits that those who are born with infirmity are those out of favor with God. And so, the sick, the poor, and the afflicted are forced to the fringes of society where they become easy targets. Second, we will notice how, again, Jesus works toward reconciling the outcasts back into right relationship with the community. He gives freely and expects nothing more than for others to trust in him and live their lives in peace. When he does this though, those who cling to their presupposed theologies and notions of righteousness will not take too kindly to him.

THE BLIND SHALL SEE

You have been blind your entire life. Not a glimmer of light or single hue has ever graced your eyes. And because of this, your people have rejected you. They have kicked you to the curb where you have led a life of poverty, forced to beg for any and everything—from scraps of food to an occasional coin. But people rarely give. Because of your infirmity, you are viewed as a sinner. And sinners are under God's curse. The Scriptures clearly state as much! (Exod 15:26, Deut 7:12–16; 28:15, 20–24, 59–60)

One day though, you meet a man named Jesus, who is being followed by a group of disciples. While in your presence, you overhear him teaching his followers "neither this man nor his parents sinned" (John 9:3). Immediately, you are stunned. You have never heard such a thing before. Time after time, throughout your entire life, you have been accused of the opposite. Even all of the scriptural evidence is stacked against you. But this teacher is saying something different, which, to say the least, is a welcomed relief.

After Jesus' attempt to reorient his disciples' worldview, he does something that is nothing short of miraculous. After uttering how he is "the light of the world" (John 9:5), he spits on the ground, making mud out of his saliva, and then spreads it onto your face. After you wash yourself at a nearby pool, a flash of brilliant, white light appears. It overwhelms your eyes, which are like those of a newborn. You squint and strain and blink until finally, things start coming into focus. And then it hits you and you are overtaken with emotion. *I can see!* As you weep uncontrollably, you start to laugh in front of all of your neighbors. "It is a miracle!" you yell.

You cannot help but tell the questioning people about the man who had just given you sight for the first time. Surprisingly, this news divides the people, and so they take you to the Pharisees for an answer. In your mind, you sarcastically think: *What answer do they need? I was blind but now I see!* But you go anyway …as if you really had much of a choice.

Being that this was a Sabbath day, and as the Scriptures clearly state that no work was to be done on a Sabbath (Exod 20:10), the Pharisees were not in a good mood when you were placed before them. In spite of your testimony, the elders only become more and more agitated. Referring to Jesus, one of them exclaims: "This man is not from God, for he does not observe the Sabbath" (John 9:16). Another, being as upset as any, yells: "How can a man who is a sinner perform such signs?" (John 9:16) But you don't care if it is a Sabbath or not, you remain convinced and convicted—"He is a prophet" (John 9:17).

The Pharisees refuse to listen. No matter how much evidence you provide them, they continue in their disbelief. Eventually, they drive you from their presence. They are convinced that not only are you a sinner but so too was this Jesus. But you knew the truth. And when Jesus finds you after you had been driven out by the Pharisees, you make sure to let him know that you believe that he is indeed the "son of man." As far as you know, nobody who had been born blind had ever had their eyes opened by another—not until now, that is. So, of course you believe. How could you not?

The theology of both the disciples and the Pharisees—born out of the devil, or, "the father of lies," as Jesus puts it in John 8:44[25]—so strongly states that "those who are afflicted with disease and sickness are sinful and thus, cursed by God." In John 9:2, Jesus' own disciples even ask, "Who sinned, this man or his parents, that he was born blind?" Before the Pharisees drive this blind man away, one of them states "You were born entirely in sins" (John 9:34). This presupposed retributive theology—where God blesses the righteous and curses the sinful—is what we discovered throughout the book of Job. In chapter 4, we explored how everyone (including Job himself) believed Job's misfortunes were due to his wickedness and God's subsequent cursing. We find this same *quid pro quo* understanding of God in Deut 28.[26]

- Deut 28:15: "If you will not obey the Lord your God by diligently observing all his commandments and decrees, which I am commanding you today, then all these curses shall come upon you and overtake you."

- Deut 28:20–24: "The Lord will send upon you disaster, panic, and frustration in everything you attempt to do, until you are destroyed and perish quickly, on account of the evil of your deeds, because you have forsaken me. The Lord will make the pestilence cling to you until it has consumed you off the land that you are entering to possess. The Lord will afflict you with consumption, fever, inflammation, with fiery heat and drought, and with blight and mildew; they shall pursue you until you perish. The sky over your head shall be bronze, and the earth under you iron. The Lord will change the rain of your land into powder, and only dust shall come down upon you from the sky until you are destroyed."

- Deut 28:59–61: "The Lord will overwhelm both you and your offspring with severe and lasting afflictions and grievous and lasting maladies. He will bring back upon you all the diseases of Egypt, of which you were in dread, and they shall cling to you. Every other malady and affliction, even though not recorded in the book of this law, the Lord will inflict on you until you are destroyed."

Now, enter Jesus, who, upon meeting the blind man, immediately corrects his disciples, who presuppose the man to be a sinner due to his condition. Then, Jesus makes a very clear statement as to what his mission is and who his mission is from in John 9:4: "We must work the *works* of *him* who sent me while it is day; night is coming when no one can work" (emphasis mine). The goals of the works Jesus speaks of are *healing* and *reconciliation*—done for those in need of it most. They are the healing of the *blind beggar*, and of a *leper* (Luke 5:12–16), a "sinful" *paralytic* (Luke 5:17–26), and a centurion's *servant* (Luke 7:1–10). They are the forgiveness of a woman caught in *adultery* (John 8:1–11). They are the feeding of 5000 *hungry* people (John 6:1–15). They are even the turning of water into wine when the party needs it most (John 2:1–11). These are works that are wholly for others, an altruistic giving of one's self for the benefit of another. The one who sends Jesus then, is the Father who—unlike the God of Deut 28, Job's friends, the Pharisees, and even the disciples at this point in the story—"sends rain on the righteous and on the unrighteous" (Matt 5:45).

That being said, now we will finally be journeying toward the Passion narrative. This will be the place where Jesus *fully* breaks open the myth that God endorses violence and in doing so, also offers himself as a model of imitation (*positive mimesis*) that, if followed, can lead to true peace—not a *Pax Romana* type of peace through state-sponsored violence; or peace through a violent interpretation of Torah, but true peace, from the giving of one's self for the other. This is the theological-anthropological revelation Anthony Bartlett describes.

To be certain, while Jesus in fact inspired countless people to follow him, he also ruffled many feathers. And while it was often due to theological differences between him and his Jewish interlocutors, it was only a matter of time until feathers became ruffled on the larger political landscape as well. And, because of this—and in spite of Jesus' best efforts to avoid such a thing—it would then be only a matter of time until Jesus would see the writing on the wall, so to speak.

THE PASSION OF THE CHRIST

SETTING THE SCENE

As we noted in the opening section of this chapter, any threats to Rome's political goals were immediately trounced by Caesar and his legions of Roman soldiers. The Jewish understanding of kingship and messianic expectation was seen as one of these threats. Jesus knew this and that is why, for instance, when the people want to make him king in John 6:15, he heads into the mountains to be by himself. He wants to distance himself from this sort of thing, where Jewish deliverance is expected to be by force. He knows where this mob of people will lead him, against his will no doubt. And the end-game of a violent revolution—that Jesus speaks of in Matt 24—would be the end of the world as they knew it.

How Jesus defines Himself and His Mission

While Jesus will indeed accept his premature death (which we will get to in just a moment); it was not his desire. His desire was to serve others, no matter the resistance he received. That is why, I believe, instead of referring to himself as the politically, and often violently, charged "messiah," his favorite self-designation was "the son of man."[27] This is an important distinction.

What this phrase "the son of man" signifies is what it means to be truly human, which, as we explored throughout this chapter, is defined by Jesus' non-violently giving of himself freely and wholly to the other for the sole purpose of healing and reconciliation. Mark 10:45 puts it thusly: "For the Son of Man came not to be served but to serve, and to give his life a ransom for many." By him using the phrase "son of man," he is telling us that he represents all of humanity, and is *for* all of humanity. Michael Hardin explains Jesus' intentions in using this designation:

> I do not think it [the phrase "the son of man"] was used as a title like "Messiah" or "High Priest' but, in keeping with the notion of corporate personality…functions as a reference to all human beings. But I will qualify that: For Jesus, the awkward phrase "son of man" (literally "the son of the man") is a reference both to himself as the "True Human" and to restored humanity as a whole.[28]

Another instance where Jesus uses the phrase "the son of man" is while standing before the high priest, and asked if he is "the Messiah, the Son of the blessed One" (Mark 14:61). He does not simply answer "yes," but refers to himself as "the son of man seated at the right hand of the Power, and 'coming with the clouds of heaven'" (Mark 14:62). Again, this is not to say that Jesus refuses to internally accept the title of "Messiah," but rather, that he does not accept any of the common understandings of it, which, as Hardin points out, are "over laden with militant and zealous baggage."[29] Instead, Jesus basically redefines the *power* associated with "Messiah," saying that power is given to the "son of man," the one who gives his life for the other (just like the suffering servant also does in Second Isaiah).

Skandalon

Because Jesus' mission is defined by his freely giving of himself for others, he eventually and quite clearly foresees his fate, which is his violent death at the "hands of those outside the law" (Acts 2:23). Jesus, though, wants it to be on his terms, and not because he gave anyone a reason to believe that he was coming as a violent revolutionary to deliver an entire population of people. Yet, the crux of it was that Jesus' terms could not be understood by others, including even his disciples. In fact, Peter—the "rock" the church is to be built upon (Matt 16:18–19)—does not even seem to "get it." In Peter's mind, violence was the only way to peace—to deliverance—to "the kingdom of God," one could say.

As he did in Mark 10:45, in Mark 8:27–33, Jesus explains his mission in terms of both the son of man and the suffering servant. It is at this point where Peter rebukes Jesus (see also Matt 16:21–23). For Peter, there is no way that the Messiah is going to suffer and then die. To that end, he tries to stop Jesus. But in that moment a potential rivalry is born. You see, as Jesus states over and over, he only speaks and does what God the Father says and does (John 5:19–20; 6:38; 8:28; 10:29; 12:49). To put it in Girardian terms, Jesus' only *model* is the Father. So for Peter to attempt to thwart that—by essentially saying to Jesus, "No, follow my way instead"—is a rather dangerous notion. Girard elucidates why this is:

> Instead of imitating Jesus, Peter wants Jesus to imitate him. If two friends imitate each other's desires, they both desire the same object. And if they cannot share this object, they will compete for it, each becoming simultaneously a model and an obstacle to each other. The competing desires intensify as model and obstacle reinforce each other, and an escalation of mimetic rivalry follows; admiration gives way to indignation, jealousy, envy, hatred, and, at last, violence and vengeance. Had Jesus initiated Peter's ambition, the two thereby would have begun competing for the leadership of some politicized "Jesus movement." Sensing the dangerous deception, Jesus vehemently interrupts Peter: "Get behind me, Satan, you are a *skandalon* to me.[30]

Jesus completely understands the temptation of taking on a model other than the Father. We witness this when he is in the wilderness and he is tempted by the devil (Luke 4:1–11). He has firsthand, tacit knowledge of just how enticing the satan can be and recognizes it as *skandalon*, or a stumbling block. In this case, though, it is Peter's desire to have Jesus follow him that is the *skandalon* personified. Thus, Jesus labels Peter as "Satan!" and tells Peter to get behind him. That is to say, Jesus is telling Peter to follow *him* in doing the will of the Father.

If, however, Jesus would have followed Peter, then his nonviolent mission would have failed and they would have entered into a rivalrous situation, one that would have potentially escalated toward overt violence, as Girard points out above. But if Jesus did that, then he would have been just like every other messiah-type figure before him (and after for that matter)—just another violent revolutionary. Jesus turns away from that temptation and marches on, keeping his eyes set only on the Father.

RISING TENSIONS AND JESUS AS SCAPEGOAT

After Jesus brings Lazarus back from the dead (John 11:1–44), the people are once again divided. Surely, many believe in him. However, others do not. And so they turn, yet again, to the Pharisees for an answer. And their answer, at last, is that Jesus must die. And not only must he die, but he must die as a scapegoat. *First*, he is blamed for the future destruction at the hands of the Romans (John 11:48), ironically the same destruction Jesus warns about on numerous occasions. *Then*, the solution to this "coming destruction," according to John 11:49–50, is to kill the "one" to spare the "all." The high priest Caiaphas proclaims, "You know nothing at all! You do not understand that it is better for you to have *one man* die for the people than to have *the whole nation* destroyed (emphasis mine)." *One man for the whole.* This is exactly how the scapegoating mechanism works. It is how it has always worked.

Jesus understands this truth about humanity. It is why he speaks of his own future death in the way that he does. In Matt 23, he attaches his death to the deaths of those who came before him (and even those who would follow!). Verses 29–36 reads like this (emphasis mine):

> Woe to you, scribes and Pharisees, hypocrites! For you build the tombs of the prophets and decorate the graves of the righteous, and you say, 'If we had lived in the days of our ancestors, we would not have taken part with them in shedding the blood of the prophets.' Thus you testify against yourselves that you are descendants of those who murdered the prophets. Fill up, then, the measure of your ancestors. You snakes, you brood of vipers! How can you escape being sentenced to Gehenna? Therefore I send you prophets, sages, and scribes, some of whom you will kill and crucify, and some you will flog in your synagogues and pursue from town to town, so that upon you may come all the righteous blood shed on earth, from the *blood of righteous Abel* to the *blood of Zechariah* son of Barachiah, whom you murdered between the sanctuary and the altar. Truly I tell you, all this will come upon this generation.[31]

There is a bookending of sorts here. Jesus is attaching his death to the first murder—that of Abel—and every murder in between, as Zechariah's is the final murder recorded in the Hebrew Scriptures.[32] This is what is later meant by the phrase: "the lamb slain from the foundation of the world" (Rev 13:8).[33] It is because of how we *blindly* structure our belief systems that has Jesus slain from the start.

Notice how I emphasized the word "blindly" in the last sentence. I wanted to call attention to the fact that this structuring sacrificial mechanism is something we barely seem privy to. This is why, when Caiaphas asserts that Jesus is going to have to die (as a substitution) with only a little manipulation (i.e., Judas' betrayal in Mark 14:43–45, false testimony/gossip in Mark 14:55, as well as the accusation of blasphemy in Mark 14:63–64), the act is swiftly carried out (with the backing of the people!). How different this is from when he entered the city, where *before* Jesus is arrested, he rides into Jerusalem like a triumphant king (although on a lowly donkey, which is a subversion of how a Caesar would enter a city, namely, on a mighty war horse).[34] Yet, the crowd is behind him *all the way*. They cry: "Hosanna! Blessed is the one who comes in the name of the Lord—the King of Israel!" (John 12:13) But then the people sway like the wind. After the hasty betrayal by Judas, which leads to an arrest and "false testimony" against Jesus, *voila*, the very same crowd who triumphantly welcomed Jesus into Jerusalem will cry out, "Let him be crucified! Let him be crucified!" (Matt 27:22–23)

It is easy to see, then, just how quickly a mob can be born, as well as how powerful one can become. This is why, earlier, Jesus is able to predict Peter's denial of him (Mark 14:27–31). Notice, in Matthew's Gospel in particular, Peter's third and final denial is said to be in front of a portion of this mob—a group of "bystanders" (Matt 26:73). The power of the mob overwhelms the fearful Peter, in spite of his good intentions (as in, when he tells Jesus "I will lay down my life for you" in John 13:37). In light of Jesus' keen sense of understanding, however, Peter's denial comes like clockwork.

Now, I do not say all of this to espouse any anti-Semitism whatsoever. That is not my view nor is it the reality. My point, then, is that a mob—*any mob*—can form quickly and turn violent. It is essential to remember that while the mob was stirred up by the Jewish authorities, those in charge—the Romans—are the ultimate authority over this whole event.[35] In this light, Jesus' death is first a political act for a very specific reason.[36]

To fully appreciate the death of Jesus, we need to put it in the context of *Pax Romana*, as the incredible violence that is poured out onto Jesus is precisely how Roman peace was achieved. It was stunning in its brutality. It was a powerful statement to anyone who even dared subvert their reign. And sadly, this "peace making" was done in a most predictably dehumanizing way (like the

Suffering Servant of Isaiah). But "work" it did. There was even a uniting against a single victim as seen in Luke 23:12. "That same day Herod and Pilate became friends with each other; before this they had been enemies." Remember, the death of a scapegoat brings about peace and catharsis where there was once tension.

Yet, through it all—and this is of utmost importance when thinking about *positive mimesis*—Jesus will stand firm on the side of mercy and forgiveness, with eyes no doubt *still* fixed on his model, the Father.

FORGIVENESS UNTO DEATH

While Jesus' commitment to non-violence and forgiveness was profound and paramount during his mission, nothing quite has the profundity of the Passion narrative. Indeed, Jesus takes his command to forgive others as much as "seventy times seven" (Matt 18:22)—a subversion of Lamech's seventy-times-seven-fold vengeance from Gen 4:24—as seriously as humanly possible. Through it all, there was but one thing on Jesus' mind, "Father, forgive them; for they do not know what they are doing" (Luke 23:34).[37] Here, Jesus detaches intention from action. He speaks to the blindness[38] of what is being done to him and remains consistent to his life's mantra of forgiveness, void of an economy of exchange. That is to say, forgiveness that is free, even while being nailed to the most brutal implements of terror that humanity can muster.

Yet there remains the glaring question: *Why?* Why does Jesus do this? Why does he lay down his life? Surely, he would have had a better chance of bringing about change had he stood up and fought for himself. All of this forgiveness and mercy talk is good for what, now that he is dead?

Three days later something *will* happen that will give us the *ability* to answer those questions. What will occur will fundamentally change the way we see everything. Or, better yet, in paraphrasing James Alison, it will fully reveal both where innocence lies and the heart of divinity.[39] And that heart is 100 percent live-giving! It will be this knowledge—mind you, knowledge we could not possess without the Resurrection—that frees us from our victim-creating systems. It will also free us to truly live without the anxiety of death that aids in creating such systems. But that is not quite where we are in our journey. We'll get there in the next chapter. So, we will have to just hang out here in this awkward state—between Jesus' death and resurrection—just like the disciples did on "Holy Saturday."[40]

My point in doing it like this is so that my friend and colleague Adam Ericksen could have the chance to interject and offer his insights as to why the Passion, like other biblical stories, while on the surface smelling of myth, is in fact not. He will do so in order to provide us with an even deeper understanding of the anthropological truths found in the Gospel, which in my opinion, further comforts those, like me, who hold to the ultimate hope that is found in this narrative.

"MYTH AND GOSPEL" BY ADAM ERICKSEN

One of the best explanations of myth from the perspective of mimetic theory is found in Gil Bailie's book *Violence Unveiled: Humanity at the Crossroads.* Bailie writes, "The root of the Greek word for myth, *muthos*, is *mu*, which means 'to close' or 'keep secret.' *Muo* means to close one's eyes or mouth, to mute the voice, or to remain mute."[41]

As Matthew explored earlier, the Girardian understanding of myths is that they are ancient stories about a mob's collective murder of a victim. They are stories that mute the voice of the victim and blind us to the reality of violence by telling us that the victim was truly guilty.

The Bacchae, for instance, is a riveting example of a myth's ability to close our eyes to the voice of the victim.[42] It tells the story of Dionysus, a god of religious ecstasy, prophecy, fertility, and wine (those last two made Dionysus especially popular!).

As gods are wont to do, Dionysus demands that all people worship him…or else! Now, the ruler of Thebes was King Pentheus, who happened to be Dionysus' cousin. And after Pentheus orders the people of Thebes to refuse to worship Dionysus, watch out.

You see, the gods within mythical narratives do not react very well to disobedience, so Dionysus seeks revenge against Pentheus. He drives some of the women of Thebes mad—including the king's mother Agaue—forcing them to head to a mountain to worship Dionysus.

To summarize the rest of the plot, Pentheus believes Dionysus is a threat to the social order of Thebes. After all, look what he did to these poor women! So, in the name of peace and order, Pentheus imprisons Dionysus. Imprisonment is not enough though, as Pentheus becomes obsessed with killing Dionysus. However, Dionysus thwarts every attempt with his divine-like powers.

Soon, Dionysus gets his revenge by luring Pentheus to the women on the mountain. Once he reaches his destination, Dionysus orders the women to kill his rival. Thinking that Pentheus is actually a young lion, the women attack him. Lying on the ground, Pentheus reaches out for his mother, hoping that she will snap out of her rage and recognize him as her son. But alas, she rips her son to pieces.

Agaue returns to the castle, holding her son's head. Still under Dionysus' spell, she holds up the head, claiming she has killed a lion. Agaue's father tells her the truth that she has not killed a young lion, but instead, has killed her own son. Agaue weeps, but Cadmus says that while Dionysus was excessive, he rightly punished them, because—here's the key to unlocking myth—Pentheus was guilty.

Pentheus was guilty because myths are told from the perspective of the victimizers, not the victim. The old adage is true, "History is written by the victors." Victors want their violence to be interpreted as virtuous, so they claim their victims are guilty, and thus, rightly punished.

Notice the theology behind the myth. The gods are fueled by violence and revenge. It's a theological worldview that justifies violence.

But Matthew is right. The Bible moves us beyond myth—sometimes by setting itself up against certain mythical narratives. That is because in the Bible you hear the voice of the victim. Abel's blood cries out to God from the earth (Gen 4:10). And while Joseph's brothers unite against him in an act of collective violence, Joseph is innocent (Gen 37—50). The cries of the Hebrew people enslaved in Egypt reach the ears of God (Exod 1—19). The prophets continually speak for the poor, the widows, and the dispossessed. In the Bible, as opposed to certain myths, the victims of human culture have a voice.

Indeed, as Matthew says, on the surface the Passion smells like a myth. Pentheus is like the political rulers, Herod and Pilate, who wanted social order in the midst of chaos. The crowd is like the women, drunk with violence, chanting "Crucify him! Crucify him!" (Luke 23:21) The mythological element of collective violence is on full display in the Passion.

But notice the radical differences. The God character in the Passion, Jesus, does not orchestrate the crowd to turn against anyone, not even against his enemies. The crowd is not drunk on a desire for divine revenge. Rather, the violence in the Passion is purely human.

In mythical narratives, the gods often respond to human disobedience with revenge, just like Dionysus does. But in the Gospels—and the whole Bible for that matter (see Gen 3, 4, 8, 11, and so on)—God responds to human disobedience with radical forgiveness and mercy. The Passion—the cross—means that Christians should know this essential truth about God: *God has nothing to do with violence, but everything to do with forgiveness.* We are the violent ones, not God.

Pentheus is viewed as guilty in the Bacchae, but Jesus is viewed as innocent in the Gospels. In John 15:25, he quoted Ps 35:19 by saying, "They hated me without cause." Part of Jesus' innocence is that he did not choose to mimic the hatred of his enemies. He did not succumb to the rivalry that engulfed Pentheus and Dionysus (like when Peter challenged him). Instead, he was engulfed by the universal love of the Father. A love so universal that it included even those we call our enemies.

The Passion radically transforms our theological worldview. God is nothing like Dionysus. God is like Jesus. God is not the one who seeks revenge; rather, God is the one who forgives unto death and resurrects to offer peace. God is not the one who creates victims; rather, God is the one who listens to the voice of the victim. And it's in that subversion of myth where we discover the truth of 1 John 4:8, "God is love." And that is where the Christian finds hope.

CHAPTER 6

THE RESURRECTION AS A NEW REALITY

"One of the things that happened as a result of the Resurrection was a shift in the possibility of human knowledge. That is to say, that before the Resurrection of our Lord, there was an area of human life that was radically unknown, maybe even unknowable. And this area of human un-know-ing was laid bare, opened up, by the Resurrection." [1]

—JAMES ALISON

O ver the course of our journey thus far, we have covered a lot of ground. In the last chapter, we explored a handful of Jesus' most famous teachings and actions, taking us to and through the earth-shattering Passion narrative. In this chapter, we are going to explore the event that is the reason for all this in the first place—an event that allows us to see the intelligence behind, not merely the Gospel of Christ Jesus, but also the reve-latory aspects of the Hebrew Scriptures. That event is what we call the Resurrection of Christ. And while it too, on the surface at least, appears to be yet another myth (as people do not just die and rise again in three days), it is in fact something quite different. The Resurrection is the culmination of this myth-subverting journey we have been on throughout this book. In it we find the voice of the divine victim is, and in fact has always been, forgiveness and peace.

Now, as we just mentioned, human beings do not just die and then rise again three days later. At least, science offers no evidence of such a thing. And frankly, neither does history, at least not in any repeatable way (*sans* for the mythical narratives of various dying and rising gods).[2] But both of these facts are okay.

Allow me to explain.

Thinking scientifically, we *should* ask: *What does science have to say about things that cannot be repeated?* Isn't that one of the foundations of the scientific method? And if the Resurrection of Christ is not something that can be scientifically repeated, then are we not dealing with a different field? I believe that we are.

Now, although we do not see multiple historical accounts of resurrections (again, *sans* certain mythical narratives) and thus cannot look throughout the epochs for an analogous event as "proof," we can look to the first century and to the very striking "doctrinal mutations" that occurred immediately following the Resurrection.

As a note: I must give credit where it is due and say that the following evidence is drawn from New Testament scholar N.T. Wright's *Surprised by Scripture* (pp 46–49). In it, he points out seven Christian "mutations" as to what "resurrection" meant, in light of Jesus.

1. Whereas there were many differing beliefs about the life hereafter in late Second Temple Jewish thought,[3] after the Resurrection Christians are quite unified in thought. Wright notes, "For almost all of the first two

centuries, Resurrection in the traditional sense holds not only center stage in Christian belief about the ultimate future but the whole stage."[4] That is to say, the Resurrection was to be viewed in one way and one way only.

2. The Resurrection goes from a more fringe belief (of those who held it) to a core one for Christian belief. As Wright points out, "You can't imagine Paul's thought without it. You shouldn't imagine John's thought without it…Take away the Resurrection and you lose the entire New Testament."[5]

3. The third transformation is in regards to what, specifically, the nature of the resurrected body would be.[6] In the early Christian view, this body will be transformed, rather than simply resuscitated or made to be what Wright calls a "shining star."[7]

4. The fourth mutation has to do with the timing of the resurrection of the dead. No Jew believed that there would be a resurrection of one that is then followed by many. Rather, those Jews who believed in a resurrection believed all of God's people would, at the end, rise as one.

5. The fifth change is what John Dominic Crossan first called "collaborative eschatology."[8] That is to say, in moving toward a future resurrection of all those in Christ, i.e., all those he died for, followers of Jesus will work toward bringing about this future kingdom, grounded in the same grace and peace Jesus displayed.

6. As Wright points out, mutation number six has to do with the Resurrection also now carrying with it a metaphorical meaning, different than the lone metaphorical reference to resurrection in Ezek 37.[9] Instead of resurrection having to do with a "return from exile," it now becomes associated to the practice of baptism and holiness (Rom 6; Col 2—3).[10]

7. The last mutation is potentially the most important with regards to what we have been exploring. While the concept of a "messiah" was quite varied in the Second Temple period—meaning, not everyone envisioned the same type of messiah-figure—*nobody* believed in a messiah who would go up against Rome and subsequently "fail," being nailed to a tree for the entire world to see. The messiah was, after all, believed to be the deliverer of Israel. Thus, for early Christians to proclaim a crucified messiah, it would have taken an event such as the Resurrection to convince them. Short of that, what good would following *this* messiah be against the "almighty" Rome?

So, when looking at the immediate impact of the Resurrection, we find compelling evidence of what appears to be a once-in-a-history type of event. Later, we will explore how the Resurrection fundamentally changes the ethics of those who chose to follow this crucified one. Again, without the Resurrection, why would so many people choose to go like lambs to the slaughter during the first few centuries?

Now, with that being said, let us get back to our Jesus story, moving from Holy Saturday to Resurrection Sunday.

THE FINAL WORD SPOKEN

With Jesus having just died, the disciples no doubt felt lost. *What will happen with Rome? What will happen to us? What was the point of all this? Where do we go from here?* So much confusion, so much lost hope for this new kingdom Jesus spoke about. Wasn't following "the messiah" during the culmination of his mission supposed to be their shining moment? Were the disciples not told to "deny themselves and take up their cross and follow" Jesus? (Mark 8:34) Could it be that they failed somehow? But, all that being speculatively said, *no matter what anybody thought*, we would soon discover the truth—and the truth would set them free.

In John 20:19, the first words out of the risen Christ's mouth were "Peace be with you." Unlike Abel, who cried for vengeance from the grave (Gen 4:10), here Jesus speaks a better word (Heb 12:24)—and that word was *peace*. *Peace*, in spite of his victimization. *Peace*, in spite of the holes in his hands and his side. Then the clincher: "As the Father has sent me, so I send you." And with what does he empower them? He breathes out the *parakletos*, or simply, the Holy Spirit. In fact, he breathes upon them the same Spirit the Father gave him, attaching *that* Spirit to the type of forgiveness he just modeled days prior, "If you forgive the sins of any, they are forgiven them; if you retain the sins of any, they are retained" (John 20:23).[11] That is to say, forgive in the same way Jesus forgave, because Jesus forgave in the same way the Father does; and trust the Spirit he just provided to guide us in this forgiveness, all in the name of peace.

As we have seen, Jesus only did what he saw the Father doing (John 5:19–20; 6:38; 8:28; 10:29; 12:49). He did so in lesson, and in action, and he did so in the face of empire and religion, to the cross, through the cross, and now after the cross. From one of the last things on his lips in Luke 23:34 to the first thing uttered to his disciples as the risen Christ in John 20:19–23, forgiveness pervades. And it is this final theological reorientation that helps the disciples understand what Jesus has been teaching and preaching and doing all along. Forgiveness is free and always has been. Jesus reveals that God is not a god of retribution, he is not vengeful, nor does he endorse sacred violence of any kind. And now the disciples could see this—and they should follow suit. They could see that following the Way of Jesus was to be truly human, and that death—even death on a Roman cross—has no authority over them in the end. Rather, the Father had authority and he was the giver of life, as proven right there before them in a fully healed and forgiving Christ.

THE EARLY CHRISTIANS

With death no longer the force that it once was, Jesus' followers quite literally were led like sheep to the slaughter. And in consistent fashion, they not only refrained from using violence to resist their persecutors, but they offered forgiveness in the same way their model, Jesus Christ did. In Acts 7:54–60, we read of the stoning of Stephen, who, just before dying, offers his spirit to Jesus and cries out: "Lord, do not hold this sin against them" (Acts 7:60). Hegesippus, an early church chronicler, tells us that Jesus' brother James is martyred while uttering, "I beseech thee, Lord God our Father, forgive them; for they know not what they do."[12] Eusebius tells us that both Peter and Paul would suffer similar fates; Peter on a cross hung upside-down, Paul in the same manner as John the Baptist, by beheading.[13]

Later, there is the infamous persecution in Lyons, where forty-eight Christians were martyred after being arrested under false pretenses, namely cannibalism and incest.[14] Not only were they martyred, but they were also tortured in the most gruesome of ways. Catholic theologian Kenneth D. Whitehead writes:

> In Lyons, the martyrs had to be taken into the arena several times before they were finally finished off. There, they had to undergo tortures such as running the gauntlet through lines of men armed with whips and scourges; being mauled by wild beasts; and being strapped to a device called the "iron chair," on which their flesh was literally roasted. In the prison, in between appearances in the arena, they were placed in stocks and their limbs stretched.[15]

Eusebius describes the torture that befell one of the martyrs of Lyons:

> On the last day of the contests, Blandina was again brought in, with Ponticus, a boy about fifteen years old. They had been brought every day to witness the sufferings of the others, and had been pressed to swear by the idols. But because they remained steadfast and despised them, the multitude became furious, so that they had no compassion for the youth of the boy nor respect for the sex of the woman. Therefore they exposed them to all the terrible sufferings and took them through the entire round of torture, repeatedly urging them to swear, but being unable to affect this; for Ponticus, encouraged by his sister so that even the heathen could see that she was confirming and strengthening him, having nobly endured every torture, gave up the ghost.

> But the blessed Blandina, last of all, having, as a noble mother, encouraged her children and sent them before her victorious to the King, endured herself all their conflicts and hastened after them, glad and rejoicing in her departure as if called to a marriage supper, rather than cast to wild beasts. And, after the scourging, after the wild beasts, after the roasting seat, she was finally enclosed in a net, and thrown before a bull. And having been tossed about by the animal, but feeling none of the things which were happening to her, on account of her hope and firm hold upon what had been entrusted to her, and her communion with Christ, she also was sacrificed. And the heathen themselves

confessed that never among them had a woman endured so many and such terrible tortures.[16]

I could have included more instances of this early Christian martyrdom, but I feel as if it is fairly safe to assume most people recognize what following the Way was all about in the first few centuries—following the way of non-violence and radical enemy love, even in the face of persecution of the most severe kind. This may be one of the reasons as to why would-be "Christians" were discipled *into becoming* followers of Jesus. Michael Hardin teaches: "Just as a person might try on clothes in a dressing room to see how they fit, so also the catechetical process was a way of helping potential converts 'try on' the Christian life before they made the final decision to live it 'til death."[17] They did not simply "give their heart to the Lord," as Christians tend to today. Rather, they learned *how* to follow this radical ethic by practicing Christianity; by picking up their cross daily, as Luke 9:23 puts it.[18]

To see this transformation in action, we can look to no better person than Saul of Tarsus (who we now call the Apostle Paul). His encounter with the risen Christ shows both the non-violent focus of the risen Christ, as well as the transformative and reconciliatory power of his presence.

SAUL THE PERSECUTOR

Saul was what most people would consider a nasty guy. In a way, he was a terrorist. He is said to be the one behind the stoning of Stephen in Acts 7:58. In Acts 8:1–3, we also learn the following:

> That day a severe persecution began against the church in Jerusalem, and all except the apostles were scattered throughout the countryside of Judea and Samaria. Devout men buried Stephen and made loud lamentation over them. But Saul was

ravaging the church by entering house after house; dragging off both men and women, he committed them to prison.

This persecution continues in Acts 9:1–2, when "Saul, still breathing threats and murder against the disciples of the Lord, went to the high priest and asked him for letters to the synagogues in Damascus, so that if he found any who belonged to the Way, men or women, he might bring them bound to Jerusalem." Then, in an instant—that is, in a blinding encounter with the risen Christ—everything would change.

Once Saul is blinded, the risen Christ asks: "Why do you persecute me?" (Acts 9:4) The question is not about his faith tradition, or about being converted to "Christianity," but rather, his sacred violence. It was about his exclusivity. It was about his "us vs. them" worldview that led him to become a murderous zealot. But this zeal would be no match for the power of the peaceful and reconciling Christ.

After Saul is sent on his way, he arrives in Damascus, still blinded by his encounter. Then, Ananias (a follower of Jesus) lays hands on him and, in the same spirit of forgiveness and *shalom* given to the disciples in John 20:19–23, welcomes Saul as a *brother*. When the scales fall from Saul's eyes so that he finally sees, Saul is powerfully reconciled into the blessed community—and henceforth, the persecution would cease. Because of the radical encounter with the forgiving Christ and the blessed community, the system of sacred violence Saul had so much zeal for would forever be disavowed, giving birth to arguably Christianity's most influential thinker.

We will return to Paul later to unpack some of his writings, as they have caused the church quite a bit of confusion and frustration. They are, after all, as 2 Pet 3:16 states, "hard to understand." So, our interpretation of Paul here will no doubt be one of many. However, based on Paul's encounter and his radical shift toward peace, I believe our reading will be an apt one. But now, let us shift gears a bit and turn our attention to how this Resurrection event—centered on the forgiving Christ of course—is not only the culmination of the journey toward a non-sacrificial, non-retributive theological reorientation and, not only an event that radically transformed the lives of countless first-century followers, but is also the true antidote for our death anxiety which Ernest Becker argues is the primary reason for the violence our world is shrouded in—one that strikes a death blow to competing immortality systems.

IMMORTALITY SYSTEMS VS. THE RESURRECTION

"Death has been swallowed up in victory. Where, O death, is your victory? Where, O death, is your sting"

–ST. PAUL IN 1 COR 15:55

Earlier, we discussed how our immortality systems are all about protecting one's idea of the heroic self. They are in place to repress death, *for we could never imagine death befalling us*, "the heroes of the cosmos," as we like to think of ourselves. But, as we have discovered, the Passion and the Resurrection is all about the pouring out of one's self for the other, in the spirit of love, mercy, compassion, and forgiveness. But this "pouring out" that Jesus displays has nothing to do with the "defense of the immortal self," as one would expect to find with an immortality system. Rather, with Jesus, it is a giving up of one's self to *those very systems*, and trusting the Way of preemptive forgiveness, even to the people within these systems who declare themselves to be his enemies. The Resurrection, no doubt, follows in this same spirit—one of forgiveness and peace (John 20)—and in doing so, gives others the strength and courage needed to trust in this Way.

This is one of the primary points of the encounter between the risen Christ and the disciples on the Emmaus road in Luke 24. After reorienting the two men's approach to the Scriptures—highlighting suffering as a key interpretive lens[19]—Jesus enters town and shares a meal with the disciples. Then, in a highly symbolic way, he blesses and breaks the bread (which represents his body). Handing it to the men, their eyes are opened and they can see. They not only see Jesus: they see his Way. And thus, it can become their Way—which is a Way that exchanges sacred violence for a communal meal. As we discovered earlier in this chapter that is exactly what happened in the first few centuries. Without this encounter—or any encounter with the risen Christ for that matter—would the disciples have remained blind to the truth? Would Jesus' message have been lost, a pointless endeavor, especially when confronting the great "immortality system" known as Rome? Indeed, I believe it would have been.

More than merely a post-Resurrection reality, Jesus spends much of his time during his three-year mission, tearing down the systems that are centered on "us over them" thinking, the type of thinking that leads to a defense of one's immortality system. He does so in three ways. Let's recap them.

First, he breaks down barriers with what he teaches in places like Matthew 5, where he declares that God does not bless some and curse others, but rather, that he "makes his sun rise on the evil and on the good, and sends rain on the righteous and on the unrighteous" (Matt 5:45). Second, Jesus was constantly working toward reconciling those on the fringes of society (scapegoats) with the group at-large (the community). In John 8, Jesus forgives a woman caught in adultery and gives her the chance to reconcile with her husband and her culture. In John 9, Jesus heals a blind man who was viewed as a sinner due to his condition and, thus, was forced to be a beggar. Lastly, Jesus then confronts those primarily responsible for the cultural scapegoating—the judgmental authorities of his day—by using their theological arguments against them.[20] He has a way of aptly pointing out hypocrisy, not only to the Pharisees who attempt to have the adulterous woman stoned in John 8, but then most dramatically throughout Matt 7 and 23. What he is constantly doing is reorienting people's worldview, and declaring that nobody has the right to accuse and condemn others, for if they do, they themselves stand condemned by their own tongue.

In this way, we must view the Resurrection as a continuation of who Jesus of Nazareth was prior to his death. In terms of character, there is no difference between the two. So we must never separate who the risen Christ is from who first-century Jesus was. Assuredly, it is he who is resurrected because it is he who poured himself out and endured the cross. And so, because we fail to find any defense of an immortality system in Jesus, but rather, a peaceful and forgiving handing over of himself and acceptance of his mortality, we come to the conclusion that Becker was in fact incorrect in his assertion that the Resurrection of Christ is just another manmade tale we tell ourselves to deny our own mortality. It is so much more than that. The Resurrection, like the Passion, is God's subversive answer to these manmade tales.

OUR NEW REALITY

Through the Resurrection, we come face to face with a new reality—that in God there is no retribution, only peace. Moreover, this new reality powerfully portrays the death of death. When Jesus returns from the dead in the same peaceful manner in which he died, the fear and anxiety over death becomes nullified—not because of some tale or mythology we concoct in order to protect our idea of the immortal self, but instead due to the reality that death itself has been conquered. In other words, the mythological immortality systems we create and violently defend crumble, for we have no reason to defend anything any longer.

This now becomes our new reality, where death is no more and there is only life. And because this was all revealed to the disciples and then passed along through what is called the apostolic witness, we have a working model to use in bringing about the peace Jesus worked so hard for. We have a chance—an obligation—to use this model in working toward ending our violent systems of immortality, our mechanisms of sacrifice, and our structures of power that require an endless stream of victims in order to prosper. And if we do, we have the promise that we will taste what the kingdom of heaven is like, both in the here and now, as well as into the forever.

Now, up to this point we have spent little time addressing the nature of the afterlife. We will do that now, by turning to St. Paul in order to explore what the eschatological implications for humanity are in light of this kind of Gospel. My greatest wish is this hopeful vision will be a "balm for healing"—not only for us individually, but also interdividually. That is to say, what happens to others in the end is just as pressing as what happens to "me." Or, as Paul so earnestly put it in Romans 9:2–3, "I have great sorrow and unceasing anguish in my heart. For I could wish that I myself were accursed and cut off from Christ for the sake of my own people, my kindred according to the flesh." And if we are in fact to pour out our love—the greatest thing we possess (1 Cor 13:13)—onto even our enemies, as Jesus commands in Matt 5:44, then their fate is just as important as ours'. To have hope in even their restoration and reconciliation is to have hope that our present life, lived in the Spirit of preemptive forgiveness, has a greater purpose, namely, to be a kind of first fruits that points to the whole harvest so that God may be all in all (1 Cor 15:28).

Not everyone will be able to draw the same hopeful conclusions we will discuss and that is okay. For myself though, what we are about to discuss has had a profoundly peaceful impact, as it is much harder to commit any type of violence against someone whom you believe will be sitting across the eternal banquet table from you. To put it in theological terms, my doctrine of universal inclusivity has informed an ethic of universal pacifism. Furthermore, it is also much more difficult to hold grudges of any kind, as it is impossible to justify not forgiving others whom you believe are already forgiven by God. And I know I am not the only one, so I encourage you to have an open mind.

So with that, here we go.

PART III
THE IMPLICATIONS

CHAPTER 7

THAT ALL MAY BE SAVED

"For it is evident that God will in truth be all in all when there shall be no evil in existence, when every created being is at harmony with itself and every tongue shall confess that Jesus Christ is Lord; when every creature shall have been made one body."

—GREGORY OF NYSSA

"In the present life God is in all, for his nature is without limits, but he is not all in all. But in the coming life, when mortality is at an end and immortality granted, and sin has no longer any place, God will be all in all. For the Lord, who loves man, punishes medicinally, that he may check the course of impiety."[1]

—THEODORET THE BLESSED

So far, we have not touched on the writings of the Apostle Paul. In this chapter, that will all change, as we will be taking a bird's eye look at a number of passages from his many letters. We will be doing so for a couple of reasons. First, not only is Paul widely regarded as Christianity's most influential thinker, but also his letters simply account for such a large portion of the Christian Scriptures—so it would be simply irresponsible not to engage his writings further. Second, Paul is the one who is *primarily* responsible for thinking about Christian theology in logical, rational, and systematic ways. So if we are going to take what we have been exploring throughout Part II, most specifically with regards to the life, death, and resurrection of Jesus Christ, and then logically think about the implications for all of humanity, then we are going to have to turn to Paul, as I believe he is our greatest resource.

FOR PAUL, *ALL* MEANS *ALL*

In chapter 6, we took a look at how Paul encountered the risen Christ and what effect that had on him. Remember, this was not merely some religious conversion—for example, from Judaism to Christianity—but a complete transformation from violent religious zealot to devout follower of the non-violent Lord. I mention this because all too often, Christians get a hold of Paul's writings and then argue for an interpretation that either takes no account of, or completely contradicts, this personal context. As we will later discuss, when interpreting something like Paul's use of the phrase "the wrath of God" many opt for a flat interpretation of that passage. God's wrath is thought of in strictly human terms; namely, in terms that include vengeance and retribution. But given Paul's single encounter with the living Lord, how does this interpretation square with Paul's experiential knowledge of God? Moreover, doesn't a God of wrath sound like the one Paul *used to* believe in, the vengeful God who would have no doubt endorsed the stoning of the "blasphemer" Stephen? Of course it does! So, I believe it behooves us to have a thorough understanding of Paul's conversion so that we do not find ourselves outside of the context of his personal encounter with the risen Christ.

The correct context, then, is one that puts Christ in the driver's seat of salvation. Christ initiates and we respond—and we can do so because it is a deliverance of God, one that causes the scales to fall from our eyes.

So, all that being said, let's explore a variety of passages that I believe point to the fact that all humans will receive the same pure act of grace that Paul himself *received* and thus, will one day (either in this life or the next) be reconciled to God.

ROMANS 5:12-19

Therefore just as one man's trespass led to condemnation for all, so one man's act of righteousness leads to justification and life for all.

–ROM 5:18

In Rom 5:12, Paul begins with what appears to be an Aristotelian logical sequence. He states:

1. Adam's sin lead to death.

2. All have sinned.

3. Therefore, death spread to all people.

In this progression, Adam is viewed as a corporate figure, as he is directly attached to the sin and death every human being experiences. Notice, then, that in verse 14, Paul intentionally makes a parallel between Adam and Christ when he says that Adam is a type of "the one who was to come." So like Adam, Christ is envisioned as a corporate figure. Now, although Adam and Christ are paralleled, Paul then argues in verse 15 that what Christ offers, namely a free gift, is going to be different than what Adam brought to all, which of course was sin and death. In fact, Paul will go on in that verse to weigh the free gift as "much more" than the sin and death Adam introduced into the world. I will note that what Paul is doing here is employing something called *argumentum a fortiori*, which seems to be a forerunner to a rabbinic hermeneutical method called "kal va-chomer."[2] When he does this, it is to place emphasis on the thing that is "much more," namely the second clause that naturally follows from the first which. In this case, that which is "much more" is the free gift of grace.

We should not fail to notice that in verse 15; the language to describe those who sinned and those who receive grace is slightly dissimilar to verse 12. Instead of using the more inclusive sounding "all," Paul uses the word "many," but again makes a strong parallel between Adam's sin and Christ's grace. Sin and death abounds to "many"—which, unless Paul is contradicting himself, is in fact all—but how *much more* does the grace of Christ abound to that very same "many."

In verse 18, Paul concludes his argument stating, "Therefore just as one man's trespass led to condemnation for all, so one man's act of righteousness leads to justification and life for all." Now, some may point back to Paul's use of the word *lambanō* in verse 17, and argue that one must actively "receive" Christ's grace in order to "be saved." However, this interpretation has three problems.

1. First, when thinking about Paul's Damascus road event, what did Paul actively do with regards to *receiving* Christ's grace? If you may recall, it was Christ who blinded him, Christ who confronted his persecution, and then Christ through Ananias who welcomes Paul into the "Christian" community. Remember, it is Ananias' "brother Saul" that causes the scales to

fall from Paul's eyes. Therefore, did Paul *really* have a choice as to whether he would receive this grace?

2. The second issue with this interpretation of "receive" is that one would have to take a single verse—actually, a single word—out of the overall thrust of Paul's argument from vv. 12–19. That is to say, setting both Adam and Christ up as paralleled corporate figures seems irresponsible if Adam's death affects a greater number of humans than Christ's free gift of grace (as many Christians contend there will be those who do not actively receive it).

3. Lastly, throughout Paul's writings, when he uses the Greek verb *lambanó* in conjunction with a divine gift of some kind, the receiver is always passive.[3] Philosopher Thomas Talbott puts forth these examples: "When Paul declared, 'five times I have received (active voice)…the forty lashes minus one' (2 Cor 11:24), we understand that he received these thirty-nine lashes in the same passive sense that a boxer might receive severe blows to the head; and when he spoke of those who 'have received (active voice) grace and apostleship to bring about the obedience of faith,' (Rom 1:5), we again understand that such persons are the recipients of some divine action in the same passive way that a newborn baby receives life."[4]

So, given the evidence—Paul's first-hand conversion experience as well as the self-evident tenor of the argument he presents in vv 12–19—we would have to conclude that throughout this passage, *all* means *all*, all of the time. Thus, just as one man

(Adam) caused all to sin and die, so too will one man (Christ) give life to *all.*

ROMANS 11:25-33

For God has imprisoned all in disobedience so that he may be merciful to all.

—ROM 11:32

Many folks—primarily Calvinists—point to a specific passage from the book of Romans to argue in favor of an exclusivist theology. Romans 9:22 reads, "What if God, desiring to show his wrath and to make known his power, has endured with much patience objects of wrath that are made for destruction." Clear, cut and dried, right? God created some in order to pour his vengeance and wrath upon!

Well, not so fast.

Notice how these "objects of wrath" are later described by Paul. In Romans 11:28, these "non-elect," who Paul, in Romans 11:26 states will indeed be saved, are described in two ways. First, per the Gospel, "they are enemies of God." I have heard no dispute from anyone regarding this. However, second, as per "election"—that is to say, as per the argument at-hand—they are to be considered "beloved," and that is because, and unlike Calvinists would contend, they are beloved by the all-merciful Father. So, their "destruction"—like Saul's—needs to be thought of in this context, rather than outside of it. Remember, Paul states earlier, in Rom 5:8: "God proves his love for us in that *while we still were sinners* Christ died for us." (emphasis mine) That is to say, while we were objects of wrath, Christ displays God's love toward us by laying down his life for us.

It is quite striking, then, that in spite of this and other instances where Paul writes that even the "elect" were at one point "children of wrath,"[5] many of those same "elect" still hold to an Augustinian exclusivism, where it has been predestined that some are "in" while others are "out." Yet I am not so sure this is what Paul is saying. What I believe he is saying is that all of us, even "the elect," will end up being both "vessels of wrath" and "vessels of mercy." To use an analogy, could we not consider Saul a "vessel of wrath," while Paul a "vessel of mercy?" Talbott explains how our subjective experience is the lens with which we interpret something like "God's wrath:"

> In Paul's scheme of things, therefore, the vessels of wrath, no less than the vessels of mercy, are objects of God's mercy, it is just that, for a person's own good, God's purifying love sometimes takes a form that a sinner will typically experience as wrath.[6]

When we refuse to live in love and refuse to live in the spirit of grace and forgiveness, we will experience God as wrath. But, through the context that "God is love" itself, it is in fact mercy. That is why I believe Paul then concludes his entire "argument" from Rom 9–11 with:

> Just as you were once disobedient to God but have now received mercy because of their disobedience, so they now have been disobedient in order that, by the mercy shown to you, they too may now receive mercy. For God has imprisoned all in disobedience so that he may be merciful to all. O the depth of the riches and wisdom and knowledge of God! How unsearchable are his judgments and how inscrutable his ways! (Rom 11: 30–33)

If you recall, we discussed how the death of Jesus represents all of humanity's judgment against God, but in contrast, the peace and forgiveness the Resurrection brought was God's judgment for humanity. So, in light of this, is it any wonder Paul declares that God's judgments would be unsearchable by the hearts of man?

They are unsearchable precisely because of the radical mercy with which God answers humanity's mimetic violence.

1 CORINTHIANS 15:22-28

For as all die in Adam, so all will be made alive in Christ.

–1 COR 15:22

Quite similar to Rom 5:18, Paul, starting in 1 Cor 15:22, again makes a parallel between the corporate figures Adam and Christ—"a man from the earth" and "a man of heaven" respectively (1 Corinthians 15:47). 1 Cor 15:22 reads: "For as all die in Adam, so all will be made alive in Christ." In vv. 23–24, Paul goes on to flesh out the details of how this will happen, "But each in his own order: Christ the first fruits, then at his coming those who belong to Christ. Then comes the end, when he hands over the kingdom to God the Father, after he has destroyed every ruler and every authority and power." Talbott interprets this passage in the following manner:

> After informing us that "in Christ shall all be made alive," Paul went on to say, "But each in his own order" (v 23). It is as if he had in mind the image of a procession and then quickly listed three segments of the procession. At the head of the procession is Christ, the first fruits; behind him are those who belong to Christ at the time of his coming; and behind him are those at the end of the procession, which is the third and final stage of Paul's "each in his own order."[7]

This was also how I interpreted this passage in *All Set Free*. And while I believe it is a solid interpretation, I now tend to lean toward an alternate one, namely one that interprets the processional as follows: Christ the first fruits, those who belong to Christ (the same everybody that are in Adam), then the end, which is when Christ destroys all rulers, authorities, and powers. That is to say, everyone in Christ is made alive (1 Cor 15:22) and then Christ will destroy the very concept of rulership, as all authority and power is Christ's and Christ's only. Then death itself—which stems from the violent systems of power—is destroyed in 1 Cor 15:26.

So, what does Paul mean when he mentions "death?"

When talking about death, Paul does so in two paradoxical sounding ways. First, in one sense, Rom 6:6–7 tells us that we must die in order to be freed from sin. Yet, in Rom 7:9–10, Paul says that he died once sin was revived. In other words, according to Paul, death (to your own fleshy desires) delivers you from sin but (in a spiritual sense) is the consequence of sin. So, when death, the last enemy, is destroyed, it is done for two distinct reasons.

1. The very thing we all need to do in order to live is to die to ourselves. Once we all do this, we no longer need death as a means by which we find life.

2. When we all die to ourselves and indeed find life in Christ, death, the final enemy, will be destroyed because life in Christ is eternal.

And so, only after death itself is destroyed—that is to say, once the only thing that can keep us from God is done away with—the Son will subject even himself to the Father so that God "may be all in all" (1 Cor 15:28). Not *all* in some or *all* in what's left, but *all* in *all*.

COLOSSIANS 1:15-20

Through him God was pleased to reconcile to himself all things.

—COL 1:20

173

Colossians 1:15–20 is a part of an early Christian hymn—a triumphant declaration.

> He is the image of the invisible God, the firstborn of *all* creation; for in him *all* things in heaven and on earth were created, things visible and invisible, whether thrones or dominions or rulers or powers—*all* things have been created through him and for him. He himself is before *all* things, and in him *all* things hold together. He is the head of the body, the church; he is the beginning, the firstborn from the dead, so that he might come to have first place in *everything*. For in him *all* the fullness of God was pleased to reconcile to himself *all* things, whether on earth or in heaven, by making peace through the blood of his cross. (emphasis mine)

In this passage, Paul (if he indeed wrote Colossians) again uses strong, inclusive language when describing the scope of Christ's reign. Similar to 1 Cor 15:24, in Col 1:16 Paul even declares all "thrones, dominions, rulers, or powers" as subjected to Christ. Even these "powers and principalities" that spilled Jesus' blood—and in fact have been shedding the blood of all the prophets "since the foundation of the world"—are included in the "all things" that are reconciled to him (Col 1:20).

And how are "all things" reconciled to God?

Paul offers us a glimpse: "by making peace through the blood of his cross" (Col 1:20). Remember, the peace of Jesus is pervasive throughout the gospels and is central to Paul's teaching as well. In fact, in Eph 6:15, the Gospel is called a "gospel of peace." For Paul, like the writer of the story of Joseph and his brothers, peace is the reconciliatory agent that unites others, which in this case, is humankind with God. And that peace was only possible because Jesus was the embodiment of such peace. So he is then given the name above all names and will come to have first place in everything (Col 1:18). Not some things or all things that are left, but *all* things.

THE NAME ABOVE ALL NAMES: JESUS. LORD. PERIOD!

The following is a letter I wrote to my best friend, Michael Machuga.[8] The goal of the letter was to put forth the proper interpretation of two Pauline passages that state *all* people will declare "Jesus is Lord." In it, I attempt to provide a thorough explanation of what Paul may have meant when he stated this. A brief contextual note: this is a response to Michael's claim that you do not need to "believe in Jesus" to achieve salvation.

Michael,

> Sadly, many Christians will miss the brilliance of the answer you put forth in your letter, with all of its layers and nuances, and simply cling to the final paragraph. They will hear: "a person does not need to believe in Jesus in order to be saved," and thus write off everything that you have to say on the matter of salvation. Perhaps some—like those who believe salvation is based on your "personal relationship with Jesus"[9]—may actually find a bit of "truth" in how you described the more relational types of belief, because for them, "faith without works is dead" (James 2:14–26). But, at the end of the day, they will still say that in addition to your relationship with Christ, you must ultimately declare that "Jesus is Lord" in order to be saved. Of course, this phrase then gets dwindled down to some pint-sized version of its former self, coming to mean nothing more than "Jesus is lord of my life." And so, because this seems to be the reality in Western Christianity (*broadly speaking*), that is what I am going to talk about in this letter.

> *What does it really mean for Jesus to be Lord?*

> Well, first off, this was a very politically charged statement during the first few centuries. Caesar, at least in the eyes of the Romans, was lord over everyone and everything. He established this through war and conquest, the world being his perpetual battlefield. After the Resurrection of Jesus, though, a group of followers began to subversively declare Jesus as Lord over all. And because Caesar's reign was believed to be over all, this was

quite a statement, because all means all. Thus, Jesus' lordship was over even Caesar himself, a corporate lordship in the most inclusive of ways.

So, with that proper historical context in mind, allow me to point to what the Apostle Paul had to say about the phrase "Jesus is Lord."

On two separate occasions, namely Rom 14:11 and Phil 2:10, Paul writes that all will declare "Jesus is Lord." Furthermore, they will do so while bowing their knees to Christ as well. No Christian denies this. Of course, they would then go on to say that those who bow and confess last (i.e., unbelievers who die without first saying the magic phrase), will do so as if defeated soldiers on a battlefield. Or, one could say, they will bow and confess in the same way people bowed and confessed to Caesar—begrudgingly or under compulsion. But that is the gospel according to Caesar, not of our Lord Jesus Christ.

Now, because I don't buy the stock line that some will bow and confess in an act of reluctance, like those who bow to petty tyrants, here is what I believe is the real reason for the universality of humanity's confession.

What we must first realize is that as Lord, Jesus is the only rightful judge of the living and the dead (1 Tim 4:2). And the reason is because of what happened on the cross. To put it plainly, he earned it. So, we can never separate who the risen Christ is from who the first-century Jesus of Nazareth was. In terms of character, there is no difference before and after death. We see this most notably when comparing the dying Jesus in Luke 23:34 and the risen Christ in John 20:19–23. Peace and forgiveness pervades in both places.

With Jesus, then, as our most merciful judge, how should we approach Paul's declaration that all will bow and confess Jesus as Lord? Paul himself informs us how, and does so in two ways. First, in Rom 14:11, he uses the Greek verb *exomologeó*, which not only means "to confess," but also "to give praise." In fact, in the NRSV, the text reads: "Every knee shall bow to me, and every tongue shall give praise to God." Thus, when all confess that "Jesus is Lord," according to Paul, they will be doing so with a grateful heart. They will be praising God! And why wouldn't they? After all, an all-merciful judge is a good thing, is it not? I hardly think they will praise God and then, in spite of this, be roasted for time-everlasting, or annihilated altogether, like many believe. I mean, are we talking about Jesus' Abba or the Aztec god Quetzalcoatl here?

Now, in 1 Cor 12:3, Paul also states that "no one can say 'Jesus is Lord' except by the Holy Spirit." So, it raises the question: *If no one can declare "Jesus is Lord" except by the Holy Spirit, and all will eventually do this, will all declarations not be directly because of the Holy Spirit?* Hence, could we not say that God will, through the power of the Holy Spirit, bring all people to openly give praise to God, while *freely* bowing their knees to Jesus? I believe we can.

I think this parallels with what you said in your previous letter, when you stated: "I am fully open to the idea of Jesus—or perhaps, this Cosmic Christ—working with me, in some mysterious way, to defeat sin." In the same way, the Holy Spirit will work with everyone, in some mysterious way, until they give praise to God and declare Jesus as Lord. But this won't be some "coerced" acknowledgment, as it will be the Christ in us (John 1:1–5)—or, in other words, our true identity—that freely chooses God in the end. At least, I see Paul being convinced of such.

So, when it is all said and done, whether you are correct or incorrect when you say that we don't have to believe in Jesus to be saved, I have to think all will be safe in the end. And by the way, I do think you are apt in your assessment of things. For, I must ask: What must "non-believers" such as the very Christlike Gandhi, or Sufi mystic Rumi, be saved *from*? Surely, not the Father of Jesus! Are they also not included in Christ's redeeming work on the cross? Well, if I am, they are. Or, as Danish philosopher Søren Kierkegaard once observed: "If others are going to hell, then I am going with them. But I do not believe that; on the contrary, I believe that we will all be saved."[10]

Your brother in Christ,

–Matthew

Ultimately, it is Jesus Christ's universal Lordship that gives the Christian hope. When all acknowledge him as Lord, then we will *fully* experience "thy kingdom come, thy will be done, on earth as it is in heaven" (Matt 6:10). This is exactly what our Lord asks us to pray now, in fact, for an earthly kingdom sent from heaven and centered on the free forgiveness of sins, to those while they are yet sinners. And while it is indeed at-hand—that is to say, here and now—we have hope that it ushers in a future time where everything is fully healed and restored, where those we forgive as Christ forgives us accept that forgiveness, and where all enter through the blessed gates that never close (Rev 21:25).

But a lingering question remains. With this eschatological hope in mind, what do we do in the meantime? What do we do in this kingdom that Jesus said is "at hand?" It is to this challenge we now turn.

CHAPTER 8

THE FINAL KINGDOM, HERE AND NOW

"Our Father in heaven,
Hallowed be your name.
Your kingdom come.
Your will be done,
On earth as it is in heaven.
Give us this day our daily bread.
And forgive us our debts,
As we also have forgiven our debtors.
And do not bring us to the time of trial,
But rescue us from the evil one."

–MATT 6:9-13

I did not want to conclude this book with a survey on the hypothetical happy ending to the human drama. And I say "hypothetical" because ultimately, we do not know the ending because we have not experienced it—for to truly know something *is* to experience it, as our knowledge is greater than the language we use to explain it.[1] But what we have experienced is the Gospel of peace, as Paul calls it in Eph 6:15, and based on my understanding of and more importantly my experience with that, I see only one ending for humanity—an ending where former enemies can look each other in the eye and offer forgiveness, mercy, grace, and the greatest of all these, love (1 Cor 13:13). Sufi mystic Bawa Muhaiyaddeen sums this up quite poetically in the following:

> Peace, unity, equality…when we are in one place, when we live in one place, eat in one place, sleep in one place, disappear in one place, die in one place, when our final judgment is given in one place, and when we finally join together *in heaven in one place* [emphasis mine], that is unity. Even when we go to that (final) place, we all live together in freedom as one family, one group. In this world and in the next world we live together in freedom, as one family of peace.[2]

Perhaps you will see things differently, and that is okay. But no matter how you view the end, I did not want to conclude with a discussion about it because, as my best friend Michael Machuga says, "Any religion worth your time will tell you that heaven is at hand." And if the heavenly life is found in Jesus— that is, in the Way of Jesus as discussed in chapters 5 and 6— then the future heaven we long for can be, in a very real way, right *now*. Jesus often said as much, when he himself said the kingdom of heaven is "at hand."[3] So I will conclude with a brief word about the reality that is in front of us now, as that is the only reality we are truly certain we have.

BE JESUS NOW

To say that heaven can be *now* is a bold statement. Not only do most Christians put heaven merely into the "other-world" category, but as we explored in chapter 1, the human experience has rarely been what we would call heavenly. Rather, for countless people, it has been quite the opposite—a living hell. And so, we recognize that we live in a sort of "in-between" state. Yes, we have hope for a future time of perfect and perpetual peace, where, as the writer of Revelation explains, "he will wipe every tear from their eyes. Death will be no more; mourning and crying and pain will be no more, for the first things have passed away" (Rev 21:4). But in the meantime, we obviously have work to do, as the eyes of humankind continue to fill with painful tears—some from the continual beating of the war drums, others from their respective culture's perpetual scapegoating and victimage, and for a litany of other reasons too numerous to list.

In fact, as I write this, the world, broadly speaking, seems to be burning around me. Sure, statistically humanity is becoming less and less violent. Yet, it does not appear that way. Syria is quickly becoming a wasteland. People are dying by the hundreds of thousands, and the solution according to most politicians and world leaders is to drop more bombs. Palestine is in a similar situation, and the same goes for places like Libya and Turkey. Due to corruption, Venezuela teeters on the edge of collapse, and sadly Brazil is not too far behind. Here in the States—where "these things could never happen"—city streets are a mess. Trust in proper policing is similar to the sixties. Blacks are getting shot by white police officers at such a rate that I am a bit surprised we have not had an outright race war in this country yet. And our politicians—most specifically the two major party Presidential candidates—are trusted by the whole of the people about as much as infamous Ponzi scheme grandmaster Bernie Madoff is. That is to say, they are not.

So we are, in a very real way, at a crossroads of sorts. With as much firepower as the world has—so much so that the entire nuclear arsenal could destroy the planet many times over—and because we are becoming more and more globalized and inter-connected, the whole thing could "blow" in an instant—like a pressure-cooker with a faulty release valve. Indeed, we have the potential to end this whole human project with a few pushes of the proverbial red button.

But again, we have hope.

We have hope because God made the decision to take part in humanity (this is what is meant by the incarnation), offering up a way out of our plight and into the kingdom of heaven.

So, how do we take part in this?

Well, as we explored in chapters 5 and 6, we follow Jesus. Now, I understand that can mean thousands of different things to thousands of different people. But what *I* specifically mean is that we will follow Jesus in his ethics. We will be decidedly non-retributive. We will be forgiving even unto death.

I fully realize that this is not easy. I struggle with it daily. Perhaps that is why, in Luke 9:23, we are told to pick up our crosses *daily*, as it is a daily struggle. I realize that what we want for our enemies, broadly speaking, is to bomb them into oblivion. Or, as former GOP Presidential candidate and self-proclaimed "face of God," Ted Cruz once put it, "We will utterly destroy ISIS. We will carpet-bomb them into oblivion. I don't know if sand can glow in the dark, but we're going to find out!"[4] I realize that entities such as ISIS, for example, are no easy demon to cast out—but you cannot cast out satan with satan (Mark 3:23). Using violence against violent entities does not work and has no place in the kingdom of heaven, which is *actually* ushered in by joining together in laying down our lives in forgiveness of the "other." It was this Way for Jesus, his disciples, and for the Christians of the first and second centuries, and so it is for us today. There are no two ways about it. As Jesus said, "Enter through the narrow gate; for the gate is wide and the road is easy that leads to destruction, and there are many who take it. For the gate is narrow and the road is hard that leads to life, and there are few who find it" (Matt 7:13–14). That is to say, violence is the easy road, but leads to destruction. On the contrary, preemptively forgiving unwarranted acts of violence is the hard road, but it leads to life.

All in all, what I want to emphasize is this: that peace can be had if only, collectively, we trust in our *true* humanness—which, being derived from the very image of the Father, is decidedly peaceful and forgiving. Jesus gave us the model with which to work and as mimetic beings, we can decide whether to follow or not. And the more we follow, the more peaceful the world becomes. In theological terms, this is what could be called a "cooperative eschatology," where the followers of Jesus aid in ushering in the kingdom of heaven. We pray for God's kingdom to come, "on earth as it is in heaven" (Matt 6:10), and then we act on it. For when the entire world comes to know the grace and forgiveness of Jesus, as testified to by the body of Christ, then heaven and earth will "collide." Perhaps then we will experience the "second coming of Christ."

May we be the "hands and feet" of Jesus and may we, as Jesus promises in John's Gospel, do even greater works than Jesus himself (John 14:12–14). So let's get to work, with peace on our hearts and preemptive forgiveness on our tongues, bringing with us the message of our Lord Jesus Christ to a hurting and lost world.

OUR PRAYER

To that end, allow me to conclude with a prayer and then a benediction. First, a prayer of peace—a cry to Abba for his Spirit to manifest in us to bring forth the kingdom of heaven, a kingdom centered on forgiveness and reconciliation.

> *Most gracious Papa, please comfort us. Heal us of our brokenness. Though we continue to structure our world through force and violence; may we all come to the realization that your kingdom is ruled by grace, love, and peace. May we all come to know that you are a God of reconciliation and restoration, that through your Spirit, we may all one day come to know and experience that. Papa; this is our most beloved hope, that we may all one day eat from the banquet table as one family.*

> *Now and always, we ask for your strength so that we may forgive others in the same way our Lord, Jesus Christ, forgives us. Give us the ability to freely give ourselves away in service of the other, that we may trust following the son of man, as we are called to do. We ask that your Spirit guides us toward meekness, toward a hunger and thirst for righteousness, toward mercy, toward purity, and toward peacemaking. May we love our enemies, may we turn the other cheek, and may we pray for our persecutors, in the same, perfect way that you do, O gracious Abba.*

> *We thank you for your peace. We thank you for your mercy, and for your grace, and truth, and love, and compassion. Continue to manifest yourself to us, in us, and through us. O Heavenly Father, your grace is awe-inspiring, and may it continue forevermore.*

> *This is our prayer. Hear us, O God. Amen.*

And now, a benediction:

The Lord bless you and keep you;
The Lord make his face to shine upon you,
And be gracious to you;
The Lord lift up his countenance upon you,
And give you peace. (Num 6:24–26)

HELL AND WRATH: THEOLOGICAL MISCONCEPTIONS AND SLOPPY EXEGESIS

"If you are not a Christian, you are going to hell. It's not unloving to say that. It's unloving not to say that."[1]

—MARK DRISCOLL

I n this essay, we are going to explore some of the more "troubling" passages found in the Christian Scriptures. We will be doing so in order to not get hung up on what are, for some, misconceptions about how to interpret these passages. After all, we would not want this beautiful Gospel we have been talking about to be distorted by some ill-conceived presuppositions. But that is exactly what many have fallen for so we need to clear the air, so to speak.

So, let us begin with an imaginative conversation between myself and a Christian who believes in the "traditional" Western understanding of hell (as eternal conscious torment). My hope is by the time we get to the end of the conversation, we will at least have a basic understanding of many of the nuances, as well as contextual considerations, that go into some of the phrases many use to argue in favor of eternal torment. Admittedly, we will not be able to cover everything in this "conversation," but hopefully we will discover that what we may have thought we knew about such things as "hell" and "eternal separation from God" just may in fact not be the case at all. And given the interdividualistic nature of humanity we have been discussing, I believe we are all going to be glad and rejoice because of it.

A MOCK CONVERSATION ABOUT HELL

Joe Christian: Matt, I've read a few of your posts on Facebook and you seem to think that everyone will be saved. How can you say that? Doesn't Jesus teach about hell more than he teaches about heaven?

Matthew Distefano: Well, no, that is actually false. My friend and colleague Dan Wilkinson tallied things up and, out of 1,944 New Testament verses attributed to Jesus, only 3 percent are potentially about hell.[2] Passages related to "heaven" come in at nearly 10 percent.[3] That being said, I don't want to skirt what I believe you are getting at. Jesus did talk about judgment and used "fiery" language, so which passage would you like to talk about, specifically?

JC: How about Mark 9:42–50? Jesus talks about tossing yourself into the sea and being thrown into hell should you continue in your sin. That seems pretty straight forward, right?

MD: Sure, but we have to back up a second and discuss the word translated as "hell" in your English Bible. It comes from the word *Gehenna*, which, in Hebrew, is a term connected to the Valley of Hinnom. It is an actual valley south of Jerusalem and was once the place where children were sacrificed to the god Molech. Second Kings 23:10 reads: "He defiled Topheth, which is in the valley of Ben-hinnom, so that no one would make a son or a daughter pass through fire as an offering to Molech."[4] Legend also has it that this valley, *Gehenna*, has a history of being a fiery trash dump in part because, after Jerusalem was destroyed by the Babylonians, the bodies of those killed were literally burned in the valley. Later, in 70 CE, in come the Romans and *wash, rinse, repeat,* Jerusalem falls again. Into *Gehenna* they go!

JC: I've heard all of that before, but isn't Jesus' usage in Mark 9 about judgment that is to be applied to the afterlife too?

MD: Yeah, I will concede that. Before I comment, though, I want to say that I believe Jesus' *primary* focus was on the *literal* destruction that was to befall Jerusalem. Jesus, among other things, was a prophet after all. And prophets often quote prophets who came before them. Jesus is no different. Brad Jersak finds evidence of this in the fact that Jesus "cites or alludes to every chapter in Jeremiah where Hinnom is mentioned."[5] And for Jeremiah, *Hinnom* was all about real destruction in real time and space by real enemies, namely Babylon.

That being said, even if Jesus *is* drawing on the Enoch tradition (1 Enoch 48:8–10, 54:1–2, 90:24–27)—which is what you allude to with your question about the afterlife—doesn't he then flip this tradition on its head in Mark 9:49–50? Doesn't Jesus, after all of the *body-part-chopping-off* talk, say that we are all going to have to pass through the fire? (And isn't it odd that nobody is suggesting Jesus wants us to literally chop our body parts off, but many then suggest that if we are not "saved," that we will end up in a *literal* fire? It seems this interpretation paints Jesus as someone who is fairly inept at making proper analogies.)

But back to the main point, doesn't Jesus say that fire produces salt in us and that this salt is actually good? Mark 9:49–50 reads: "For everyone will be salted with fire. Salt is good; but if salt has lost its saltiness, how can you season it? Have salt in yourselves, and be at peace with one another."

This would be in line, then, with how the Apostle Paul also talks about fire in 1 Cor 3:12–15, which reads:

> Now if anyone builds on the foundation with gold, silver, precious stones, wood, hay, straw—the work of each builder will become visible, for the Day will disclose it, because it will be revealed with fire, and the fire will test what sort of work each has done. If what has been built on the foundation survives, the builder will receive a reward. If the work is burned up, the builder will suffer loss; the builder *will be saved,* but *only* as through fire (emphasis mine).

So what I believe Jesus is doing in Mark 9 is subversive in nature. Jersak writes:

> Jesus began with the language of *Gehenna* from Jeremiah and Isaiah (that was about earthly destruction by foreign enemies that would result in death)—then he adopted Enoch's apocalyptic re-interpretation of those verses as an afterlife judgment in hell—then he completely subverts with his own vision where the fire is: (A) inclusive to everyone, (B) good/purifying, (C) intentional, (D) immediate in this life, and (E) internalized in the heart.[6]

According to Jesus, it's not just the "enemies" of God who go into the fire, but everybody, and, as Paul then strongly suggests, it is this *very* fire that saves the person. Remember, Jesus calls this "good" (Mark 9:50).

It's as if Jesus is saying: "Heed my warnings or you will literally end up in *Gehenna*, just like before. But also, get rid of those things that cause you to stumble, lest you risk having them burned off by the fire of the Father."

JC: Hmmm…interesting. I just hope that you are not downplaying the warnings at all.

MD: Of course not! I just think that a quick, *prima facie* reading of something like this will not suffice if we are to understand all of the layers and depth of the teaching. But I take the warnings quite seriously, affirming both the "here and now" and "after this life" implications of what Jesus is teaching here.

JC: So, do you not then believe someone has to accept Jesus in order to earn salvation?

MD: Well, personally, I do not think anyone can *do* anything in order to *earn* salvation. I believe salvation is a free gift of grace. The Calvinists would probably agree with me there. I would just then say it is given to all, not just some.

JC: But don't you think that if you choose to be wicked here in this life, that there should be consequences for that? Shouldn't there be punishment and isn't that what something like the Parable of the Sheep and the Goats teaches? In fact, doesn't this punishment last forever?

MD: Good question. First, I think there are great consequences for wickedness. Or, in other words, there are great consequences for not being loving, for neglecting the "least of these," for instance. Indeed, there are not only real-life consequences in the here and now—just look at the world around us—but also "eternal" consequences. Now, I put scare quotes around "eternal" because that is the type of "punishment" the Parable of the Sheep and the Goats mentions, and it often gets misinterpreted to mean "everlasting." Matthew 25:46 states: "And these [the goats] will go away into eternal punishment, but the righteous [the sheep] into eternal life."

JC: And doesn't that have to mean that some end up in hell, because if the eternal punishment isn't really forever, then the eternal life the righteous go to isn't forever!

MD: Sure, you *could* interpret the parable in such a way. But you would have to remember: first, the point of this parable is that those who think they are in are out and those who don't know they are in are in fact in. It is pedagogical, meant to teach us something, namely that God is more concerned with how we treat each other than showing ourselves to be "holy" in front of God. Jeff Turner sums it up nicely with a recent Facebook post:

> In the parable of the sheep and the goats we find that God considers sacred the actions of those so in love with humanity that they never even think to figure God into the equation, but vain the actions of those so enamored with God that they never think to figure humanity into the equation. Service to humanity with no religious motivation is far more Godly than service to God with no humanitarian motivation.[7]

So my question is this: are you sure that you want to argue for the interpretation you are arguing for? From the looks of things, we Christians have a long way to go when it comes to "feeding the hungry, giving water to the thirsty, welcoming in strangers, clothing the naked, and visiting the sick and imprisoned" (to paraphrase Matt 25:35–43). Second, the phrase "eternal punishment" doesn't necessarily mean what you probably think it means.

The Greek word *aiōnios* can mean eternal, but it can also mean "pertaining to an age." But for sake of argument, let's just say we translate *aiōnios* to eternal, need it imply a "minute by minute" understanding? What if *aiōnios* has more to do with the quality of something, or its nature, rather than a specific quantity or duration? Thomas Talbott offers a fitting explanation to what I am getting at:

Eternal punishment is simply punishment of any duration that has its causal source in the eternal purposes of God. As [William] Barclay himself put it, "Eternal punishment is…literally that kind of remedial punishment which it befits God to give and which only God can give."[8] We see this clearly in the letter of Jude, where the author described the fire that consumed Sodom and Gomorrah as "eternal fire."…The point here was not that the fire literally burned forever without consuming these cities and continues to burn even today. The point was that the fire is a form of divine judgment upon these cities, a foreshadowing of eschatological judgment, and that its causal source lies in the eternal God himself. And similarly for the eternal fire and the eternal punishment to which Jesus alluded in Matt 25:41 and 46 respectively: like the fire that consumed Sodom and Gomorrah, this fire will not be eternal in the sense that it will burn forever without consuming anything—without consuming, for example, that which is false within a person—and neither will it be eternal in the sense that it continues forever without accomplishing its corrective purpose. Both the fire and the punishment are eternal in the twofold sense that their causal source lies in the eternal God himself and that their corrective effects will literally endure forever. For anything that the eternal God does (or any specific action of his in the created order) is eternal in the sense that it is the eternal God who does it.[9]

JC: Okay, I'll have to chew on that some more. Can we perhaps move on and discuss another passage, namely Paul's clear message in 2 Thess 1:9, where the wicked will "suffer the punishment of eternal destruction, separated from the presence of the Lord and from the glory of his might?"

MD: Of course. Allow me to begin by writing out 2 Thess 1:7b–10 (NIV) so we can see the whole picture:

> This will happen when the Lord Jesus is revealed from heaven in blazing fire and with powerful angels. He will punish those who do not know God and do not obey the gospel of our Lord Jesus. They will be punished with everlasting destruction and shut out

from the presence of the Lord and from the glory of his might on the day he comes to be glorified in his holy people and to be marveled at among all those who have believed. This includes you, because you believed our testimony to you.

On the surface, yes, this passage seems to argue that some people will one day be shut out from God's presence and punished for time-everlasting. And if this is indeed Paul's letter—which is doubted by many scholars, but for the sake of argument we will accept it as such—then this is the only place that I can think of where Paul potentially speaks of "eternal separation from God." However, I believe this translation finds its foundation atop shaky ground.

Let me explain.

First, when Christians mention phrases like "eternal separation from God," they generally have one of two things in mind. Many describe it as eternal conscious torment, where a person is not only separated from God, but who also remains alive in order to be tormented—either with literal or figurative fire—for all eternity. Then there is a growing minority who believe the wicked will not be eternally tormented, but eternally "destroyed," or, in other words, annihilated. Metaphysically, this proposition at least makes sense, for I will concede that someone theoretically *could* be annihilated—wiped out of existence altogether—and thus be found to be "eternally separated from God." But the eternal torment model has some *especially* major issues. In a metaphysical sense, is it even possible to exist outside of God's presence, given how God is that which holds the whole of Creation together? How does one become metaphysically separated from this life source, and yet remain in "existence?" The writer of Ps 139:7–8 seems to find it an absurd proposition, proclaiming "Where can I go from your spirit? Or where can I flee from your presence? If I ascend to heaven, you are there; if I make my bed in *Sheol*, you are there." So, right out of the gates, the doctrine of eternal conscious torment where in which hell is defined as "eternal separation from God," seems like a metaphysical absurdity—that is, short of some quasi-polytheistic reality (where hell is held together by a second God or worse yet, becomes its own God in order to hold itself together).

Moreover, if you take a look at 2 Thess 1:9, specifically, you will notice that the NIV includes the phrase "shut out from the presence of the Lord." In Greek, however, the word *apo*, which is what the translators have rendered "shut out from," literally means "from," and while it can indeed mean "away from," it would have to be modified to read as such. For instance, in Rev 6:16, *apo* gets modified by the phrase "hide us," so that it is interpreted "hide us from (*apo*) the presence of him who sits on the throne."[10] The same thing goes for Isa 2:10—a verse being referenced in 2 Thess—where it reads "enter into the rock, and hide in the dust from (*apo*) the terror of the Lord, and from the glory of his majesty." But here in 2 Thess 1:9, there is no modifier. The eternal destruction (*olethron aionion*) Paul is talking about comes directly from (*apo*) the presence of the Lord. Notice the parallelism between this passage and that of Acts 3:19:

"Eternal destruction from the presence of the Lord" *(olethron aionion apo prosopou tou Kyriou)* –2 THESSALONIANS 1:9	"Times of refreshing from the presence of the Lord" *(kairoi anapsyxeos apo prosopou tou Kyriou)* –ACTS 3:19

In each case, what is coming comes from the Lord: eternal destruction (*olethron aionion*) and times of refreshing (*kairoi anapsyxeos*).

Now, let us focus our attention on the doctrine that states some will suffer annihilation, as there is the possibility that Paul indeed meant some sinners would be punished by God in such a way that they are snuffed out forever. That is to say, the *olethron aionion* they suffer from the presence of the Lord will put them out of existence altogether. So let us get dig further into the meat of the passage at hand to see if that is indeed the case or not.

In English, when we hear that someone will be "punished with eternal destruction," we generally think that their situation is hopeless. That is to say, once they are eternally destroyed, then they are done for, with no future hope of return. However, when Paul uses phrase "eternal destruction," he has something different in mind.

To show this, we will turn to his letter to the Corinthians.

In 1 Cor 5, Paul begins discussing a case of incest among the Corinthian people. He is so harsh in his critique that he describes this type of immoral behavior as "a kind that is not found even among pagans" (1 Cor 5:1). Not only does Paul recommend the person be "removed" from the church, but he also pronounces judgment in the name of the Lord Jesus on this man (1 Cor 5:2–4). He then instructs the Corinthians to "hand this man over to Satan for the destruction (*olethron*) of the flesh, so that his spirit may be saved in the day of the Lord" (1 Cor 5:5)—the same "day of the Lord," mind you, Paul is referencing in 2 Thess 1:10. So the destruction, albeit harsh, is actually what one as wicked as the Corinthian man faces in order to have his spirit saved. Or, as Paul, in his letter to the Corinthians, puts it:

> Now, if anyone builds on the foundation with gold, silver, precious stones, wood, hay, straw—the work of each builder will become visible, for the Day will disclose it, because it will be revealed with fire, and the fire will test that sort of work each has done. If what has been built on the foundation survives,

the builder will receive a reward. If the work is burned up, the builder will suffer loss; the builder will be saved, but only as through fire (1 Cor 3:12–15).

Again, on the day of the Lord, some will suffer loss—that is, destruction of the flesh (wood, hay, straw)—but through fire will be saved. They will not be utterly destroyed in the metaphysical sense, but destroyed in the same sense Saul was destroyed, where *all*—and *all* means *all*—that causes wickedness is burned up in order for the spirit to be saved.

This is the vision of God's restorative justice that Paul possessed—thus his use of the word *dikēn* in 2 Thess 1:9. While various translators have rendered this word "punishment" (NIV and RSV) and "penalty" (NASB), the most accurate translation is simply "justice." It comes from the noun *dikē*, which carries with it a judicial context. In fact, the theme of justice pervades the first part of 2 Thess. Paul even writes, "It is indeed just for God to repay with affliction those who afflict you" (2 Thess 1:6). Paul's affliction "suffered" at the hands of God's justice, then, one could say, was that he was struck blind (Acts 9:8). So, the subsequent "eternal destruction" is not simply an arbitrary punishment or penalty for wickedness, but a matter of justice.

Now, when we shift our attention to the Old Testament context (Isa 2—5), what we will notice is two-fold: justice is again a prevailing theme and those who face judgment from the Lord have a restored and hopeful ending. In fact, the prophecy in Isaiah begins by looking forward to a future time when *all the nations* shall stream to the Lord's house (Isa 2:2–3—emphasis mine). There will be no more war, as the nations will have "beat their swords into plowshares, and their spears into pruning hooks" (Isa 2:4). This will all come to pass because of the righteous justice of the Lord.

But that does not mean people are not "punished," or that justice is cheap. No! Wicked rebels will hide in terror, haughty eyes will be brought low, and pride will concede to humility (Isa 2:10–11). That is to say, the wicked will be destroyed in their ways, and they will have nothing to do but begin to seek repentance (Isa 2:18). Reconciliation is even later seen between the rebellious and the Lord in Isa 4:3–4: "Whoever is left in Zion and remains in Jerusalem will be called holy, everyone who has been recorded for life in Jerusalem, once the Lord has washed away the filth of the daughters of Zion and cleansed the blood-stains of Jerusalem from its midst by a spirit of judgment and by a spirit of burning." It is this type of justice—this purifying fire of the Lord—that leads to the hopeful vision laid out at the beginning of the prophecy.

All of that said; let us turn our attention back to Paul, and explore one last pressing matter that deserves our focus, namely, Paul's apocalyptic experiential knowledge of God's "destructive" justice. For without again mentioning his very real encounter with the risen Christ, and the very real destruction it brought him, all of our exegetical work could be moot or speculative at best. After all, no human being in history has been able to distance themself from their own subjective lens. So, when we talk about God, or anything for that matter, we are always doing so with our real-world experiences in mind (much of the time, even non-consciously). The same goes for Paul when he talks about the kind of destruction that comes from the very face of God.

As we have seen, pre-conversion Saul was a violent zealot. He was a Pharisee, and per his own words, "blameless" in terms of righteousness under the law (Phil 3:6). But he had God all wrong. Like many of his interlocutors, Saul believed that God wanted zealots, that he wanted keepers of the law, those who would commit violence for his namesake. But nay! God wanted servants of others, purveyors of grace, those who would confront violence with peace for his namesake.

As I alluded to earlier, this destroyed Saul. It destroyed his theology, his ethics, his philosophy, everything. Like the destruction of the incestuous man in 1 Cor 5, this sounds harsh. But had either man not been met with this type of destruction, where the false self is utterly burned away, they could not have been saved. Surely, having been built upon the foundation of mere wood, hay, and straw, their spirits would have died.

It is this context, then, from which Paul speaks of destruction, stemming from his tacit knowledge of what God is like as gleaned from his revelatory encounter with Christ. It is not a type of destruction that leads to utter annihilation, but a type of destruction that annihilates everything that prevents one from entering the kingdom of God. It transforms violent zealots into non-violent Christ-followers, turning murderous sinners into peaceful saints. Indeed, it is destruction of the best kind. And incidentally, it is the very sort of destruction Paul is describing in 2 Thess 1:9.

JC: Well, thanks for your input. You have given me much to think about vis-à-vis this phrase from 2 Thess. Now, let's discuss one last thing, namely the book of Revelation. Without getting into the minute details of the book, isn't it fair to say that the book paints a hopeless ending for many?

MD: The book of Revelation is a terribly difficult book to interpret. Allow me to offer what are, admittedly, only some preliminary thoughts.

First, we must view everything, including what is contained in this apocalyptic book, in light of the cross of Jesus, and not the other way around. In the following, Brad Jersak employs

Peter Enns' understanding of what is known as a Christotelic hermeneutical method—where Christ and his redemptive purposes are the end goal and thus our hermeneutical lens—to interpret Revelation:

> It is the conviction of the Apostles that the eschaton had come in Christ that drove them back to see where and how their Scripture spoke of him. And this was not a matter of grammatical-historical exegesis but a Christ-driven hermeneutic... for the church, the Old Testament (*and Revelation*) does not exist on its own, in isolation from the completion of the Old Testament story in the death and Resurrection of Christ. The Old Testament (*and Revelation*) finds its telos, its completion, in Christ. This is not to say that the vibrancy of the Old Testament witness now comes to an end, but that—on the basis of apostolic authority—it finds its proper goal, purpose, telos, in that event by which God himself determined to punctuate his covenant: Christ.[11]

Now, while some, like Pastor Mark Driscoll, are waiting for a bad-ass Jesus "with a tattoo down his leg, a sword in his hand and the commitment to make someone bleed,"[12] a Christotelic hermeneutic states that is simply not going to happen. Regardless of how imaginative and apocalyptic the whole of Revelation is, we need to keep this in mind. We also need to bear in mind the vision in Rev 5, as the writer gives clues into his very own Christotelic hermeneutic.

After John begins to weep because no one could open the scroll, he is comforted by one of the elders, who says, "Do not weep. See, the Lion of the tribe of Judah, the Root of David, has conquered, so that he can open the scroll and its seven seals" (Rev 5:5). So when John turns, he must be expecting to find a lion. But instead, he finds a "Lamb standing as if it had been slaughtered" (Rev 5:6). Like in Isa 52:15, power and authority are subverted—whereas power and authority used to be analogous with a lion, it is now given to a peaceful Lamb. This is a Lamb who, remember, offered forgiveness from the cross and after the cross, not a Lamb who will come back to kick ass and take names.

That being said, let's focus on the end of the book because in spite of all the (human caused) horror contained throughout the many chapters of Revelation, there is a hopeful ending to the drama. And so, perhaps this promising conclusion will then allow us to see the middle parts with new eyes.

Notice how, in Rev 21:24, we read that the nations are seen inside the gates of New Jerusalem—"heaven," one could say. But these nations are the bad guys. Brad Jersak aptly points out, "Throughout the first twenty chapters of Revelation, there are only two groups of people: the kings and nations who are evil and the Bride, who has come from 'out of the nations'"[13] So "nation" is not a compliment according to the writer of Revelation. Yet, in *The Evangelical Universalist*, Gregory MacDonald (Robin Parry) elucidates for his readers how these nations make the long and grueling journey toward and into the perpetually open gates of New Jerusalem (Rev 22:15),[14] highlighting five crucial stages along the way. Jersak summarizes them as follows:

1. *Immoral, Deceptive, and Dominant* (see Rev 11:2, 9, 18; 14:8; 17:2, 10–12, 15, 18; 18:3, 9, 23)

2. *Rebellious and Defeated* (see Rev 6:15; 16:12–14; 17:14, 19; 19:18–19; 20:8; Isa 34:1–2; 60:12, 20)

3. *Surrendered and Submitted* (see Rev 12:5; 15:3; 17:14; 19:15–16; Ps 2:8)

4. *Restored and Paying Homage* (see Rev 15:4, Rev 21:24, 26; 22:2; Isa 60:3, 5–9, 11)

5. *Offering Servitude and Giving Honor* (see Rev 1:5; 2:26; Isa 60:10, 13–14, 16)[15]

So in spite of the wicked nations' war against the Lamb, where in which they are defeated and tossed into a "lake of fire," they are later seen bringing "their glory into it" (Rev 21:24).

This sort of talk about wicked nations is nothing new when it comes to Jewish apocalyptic literature. In the writings of some of the prophets, these nations are often on the receiving end of God's giant foot. In Jer 48, for instance, the Moabites face all sorts of smiting. In Jer 48:4, the nation is "destroyed." Her towns become desolate in Jer 48:9, and in Jer 48:20, she is completely laid to waste—this, in the year of their punishment (Jer 48:44). Yet, the very last verse of Jer 48 reads, "Yet I will restore the fortunes of Moab in the latter days, says the Lord" (Jer 48:48). The same sort of fate befalls Elam in Jer 49. After this nation has disaster and the sword of the Lord visit them (Jer 49:37)—killing their kings and officials (Jer 49:38)—their fortunes are restored, again "in the latter days" (Jer 49:39). So yes, these nations are wiped out, burned up, laid waste, utterly destroyed, and yet, in the end, are restored by God.

Now, focusing our attention back on Revelation, anyone who in fact posthumously enters New Jerusalem *will* have to have their robes "washed in the blood of the Lamb" (Rev 22:14). That is to say, they will experience salvation in Christ—and by no other means—by taking up the call from the perpetually inviting bride (Rev 22:17) and coming through the perpetually open gates (Rev 22:15). And then, once inside, they will be able to partake of the leaves of the tree that is for the "healing of the nations" (Rev 22:2)—the very nations, with their wicked kings and leaders, who had earlier been tossed into the lake of fire.

I admit that so much more could be said about Revelation. This was but a primer on how one would approach the book in light of a Christocentric and Christotelic hermeneutic. For a more detailed survey, I recommend *Compassionate Eschatology: The Future as Friend*, edited by Ted Grimsrud and Michael Hardin, *The Evangelical Universalist* by Gregory MacDonald, and *Her Gates will Never Be Shut* by Brad Jersak.

JC: Thank you. You have given me enough to chew on for now.

MD: You are welcome.

This imaginative conversation is not meant to be the be-all-end-all when it comes to "hell" or postmortem justice/punishment. Rather, it is meant to get us to think about these matters in a broader and deeper way, as well as a more contextually relevant one. Or, as N.T. Wright famously penned, "For too long we have read scripture with nineteenth-century eyes and sixteenth-century questions. It's time to get back to reading with first-century eyes and twenty-first century questions."[16]

Now, we turn our attention to Paul's use of the phrase "the wrath of God." Our hope is to show how our reading of the non-retributive God is not at odds with Paul's discussion of God's wrath. Instead, we will discover how it is a flat reading of Paul that in fact leads to an incorrect understanding of what Paul is referring to vis-à-vis the "the wrath of God."

THE WRATH OF GOD: WHAT IS IT AND WHO IS CALLING FOR IT?

Like many Western Christian doctrines, the definition of God's wrath seems to be a given. In the most explicit of ways, it is infamously expressed by Jonathan Edwards in his sermon "Sinners in the Hands of an Angry God" as follows:

> The God that holds you over the pit of hell, much as one holds a spider or some loathsome insect over the fire, abhors you, and is dreadfully provoked. His wrath towards you burns like fire; he looks upon you as worthy of nothing else but to be cast into the fire. He is of purer eyes than to bear you in his sight, you are ten thousand times as abominable in his eyes as the most hateful, venomous serpent is in ours.[17]

Then there is this, from Mark Driscoll, one of today's most prominent Calvinist voices:

> Some of you, God hates you. Some of you, God is sick of you. God is frustrated with you. God is wearied by you. God has suffered long enough with you. He doesn't think you're cute. He doesn't think it's funny. He doesn't think your excuse is meritous [sic].[18] He doesn't care if you compare yourself to someone worse than you, he hates them too. God hates, right now, personally, objectively, hates some of you. He has had enough. He is sick of it…God doesn't just hate what you do, God hates who you are.[19]

Frankly, any eagerness to espouse such a view makes me cringe. I mean, I do understand the propensity to believe in a *quid pro quo* type of God who reserves blessings for the righteous while reserving wrath for the wicked. I do understand the human psychological need to ensure that we are "in" rather than "out," that we are *Jacob* rather than *Esau*, *elect* rather than *nonelect*, and *vessels of mercy* rather than *vessels of wrath* (Rom 9:22–23). But as we discussed earlier, in regards to mimetic desire and humanity's death anxiety, this does not mean this "in and out" thinking is "from God."

With that being said, what then do we do with this business of the "wrath of God" that the Apostle Paul talks about in Rom 1:18? Isn't it clear that Paul himself believes that "the wrath of

God is revealed from heaven against all ungodliness and wickedness of those who by their wickedness suppress the truth?" It seems pretty obvious what Paul is getting at here, does it not? Well, not so fast.

In *The Deliverance of God: An Apocalyptic Rereading of Justification in Paul*, Pauline scholar Douglas Campbell offers a radical re-reading of Romans, with great emphasis on how one should really be reading Rom 1–4. He argues that, instead of Romans 1:18–32 being the voice of Paul; it is instead the voice of the false teachers that were either in Rome or on their way to Rome.[20] Thus, in the first four chapters of Romans, Paul will be "talking through" two dissimilar gospels—one his own and the other the false teacher's.[21] Campbell explains Paul's method:

> There are certain instances where Paul attributes material to the Teacher directly, using the technique *prosopopoeia*. In these texts the Teacher in effects speaks for himself (although suitably crafted by Paul, of course)—first in the opening of his usual conversion speech (1:18–32), and then later in dialogue with Paul (3:1–9). However, for much of the rest of the argument Paul is quoting the Teacher's teaching, and rather sarcastically, and this is entirely consistent with his main rhetorical goal throughout the section, which is to refute the Teacher in terms of his own gospel.[22]

But, why would Paul write in such a way? you might ask. Well, here is how I understand the gist of it.

Paul is frankly quite peeved over the fact that there are teachers teaching a false gospel, both in churches that he founded as well as in Rome. Paul warns his readers about these teachers: "Watch out for *those* who cause divisions and put obstacles in your way that are *contrary to the teaching* you have learned" (Rom 16:17—emphasis mine). In his earlier letter to the Galatian churches,[23] he does the same thing, when he rebukes those who have swindled the Galatians by perverting the gospel of Christ

203

(Gal 1:7). To Paul, these teachers are "false believers," whose goal is to enslave those living in the freedom found in Christ Jesus (Gal 2:4).

So, who specifically are these false teachers and what was their message?

In short, they are Jewish-Christian teachers and their message is a Jewish-centered Christianity. The evidence for their identity is ample:

- In Acts 11:2–3, a group of "circumcised believers" (Jewish Christians) from Jerusalem criticize Peter for eating with "uncircumcised men" (Gentiles).

- In Acts 15:1–2, "certain individuals" teach the following: "Unless you are circumcised according to the custom of Moses, you cannot be saved." This caused dissention with both Paul and Barnabas.

- In Gal 2:11–12, Paul rebukes Peter over his refusal to share meals with the Gentiles. It is strongly implied that Peter was influenced by "certain people" who came from James (the Jerusalem church).

In addition to the observance of the laws in Torah, these teachers espouse a retributive eschatology, often strongly aimed at "pagan Gentiles."[24] That is to say, in line with the theology in places like Deut 28, the teachers teach that the righteous (no doubt themselves!) are blessed/saved, while the wicked (no doubt others!) endure God's wrath. Again, this is the *quid pro quo* God, but it is not the God of Jesus, as we discovered in chapter 5.

Now, focusing our attention back onto Rom 1:18–32, we will consider how Paul sets up both gospels in parallel fashion: his own followed by that of the law-centered, false one.

- Paul's Gospel: The righteousness of God is revealed through Christ's faith and the righteous will live by trust (v 17).

- The false Gospel: The wrath of God (*orge theou*) will be revealed against those who do not live up to a certain ethical code (v 18).

That "ethical code"—which draws heavily from the anti-Gentile Wisdom of Solomon literature—is laid out all throughout 1:18–32. And while Paul might even find fault with the behaviors listed in those verses; that is not the point of his argument.

The point is that Paul is going to then turn the false teachers' argument on themselves. In short, they are going to be deemed "hypocrites" by their own logic, as Paul states in Rom 2:1—the voice of Paul: "*Therefore* you have no excuse, whoever you are, when you judge others; for in passing judgment on another you condemn yourself, because you, the judge, are doing the very same things" (emphasis mine). What I believe the gist of what Paul is saying is: *While it may be true that there are those who indeed do the very things you accuse them of, because you are doing the same things, then you are condemned by your own standard.*

Paul then goes on. He lays out a mock-dialogue between himself and the false teacher. He does so in order to strengthen his case for his gospel and model how the false gospel of the teachers is just that, false, bogus, dead-on-arrival. Scholars call this type of argumentation "diatribe," and it runs from 2:1–4:3.[25]

What is really fascinating is the way in which Paul specifically speaks of "God's wrath" throughout his letter. In every instance after Rom 1:18, he simply uses the word *orge*, or "the wrath," rather than *orge theou*, or "the wrath of God" (see Rom 2:5; 4:15; 5:9; 9:22; 12:19; 13:4–5). That is to say, the "wrath of God" is only found in the gospel of the false teacher. In contrast, when

Paul, during his initial rebuttal in Rom 2:5, talks about wrath, he ties it to human behavior. This subtle change is crucial. Rom 2:5 reads: "But by *your* hard and impenitent heart *you* are storing up wrath for *yourself* on the day of wrath, when God's righteous judgment will be revealed" (emphasis mine). Paul Nuechterlein explains what is going on here:

> Wrath is simply "wrath" here, and no longer the "wrath of God," because it can instead be seen to be the wrath we store up for ourselves, due to our idolatry of righteous violence. On the "day of wrath," namely, the time when our human wrath comes to roost, God's righteous judgment will be revealed, precisely as something different than our wrath. It will be revealed as a love that reaches out in grace as a free gift in faith (Romans 3:21–26) even to sinners, to God's enemies (Romans 5:8–10).[26]

Now, there is one other instance—namely Rom 3:5—where "wrath" seems specifically attached to God. But even then, Paul qualifies this by saying he is "speaking in human terms." What is interesting, then, is that when Paul does speak, not in human terms, but rather, in divine terms, he speaks in terms of mercy, not wrath. Romans 11:32–33 reads: "For God has imprisoned all in disobedience so that he may be merciful to all. O the depth of the riches and wisdom and knowledge of God! How unsearchable are his judgments and how inscrutable his ways!" For Paul, the ways in which God works are so dissimilar to that of humanity, that he deems them unsearchable by human standards. The human mind, which talks in terms of wrath, simply cannot fathom the God who is wholly merciful.

Much more could be said on this topic. In fact, Campbell's tome is roughly 1,200 pages. Our purpose, then, was to simply put forth another way in which to approach "God's wrath"— one that, as we have been exploring, brings together the life and teachings of both Jesus and Paul. For each, God's wrath was nuanced. Sure, it could be seen as God giving sinners over to the consequences of their sin, and thus could be called wrathful (speaking in human terms), but it comes from an all-merciful God. Or, as Jesus himself taught, God's perfection is based on his all-merciful love (Matt 5:48 and Luke 6:36).

In the end, when we think about hell and wrath, we must keep in mind the context that God is love (1 John 4:8) and that Jesus lived, died, and came back from the dead preaching mercy, peace, and forgiveness. We can call this lens a Christocentric, Christotelic, or Cruciform hermeneutic, but no matter what label we put on it, it is Christ first, Christ last, and Christ everything in between. And it is a crucified and risen forgiving Christ, a Christ who embodied the Father's merciful love for all of humanity.

Indeed, God's mercy endures forever (Psa 136:24).

Shalom, salaam, and in the words of our risen Lord, "Peace be unto you" (John 20:21).

END NOTES

FOREWORD

1. Wright, *Surprised by Hope*, 137.

PREFACE

1. This essay can be found at https://www.ravenfoundation.org/wp-content/uploads/2012/08/The-Root-of-Violence-by-Matthew-Distefano.pdf.

2. J.J.'s tweet can be found at https://twitter.com/gaetawoo/status/670357174363680768.

3. The quote I am referring to reads in full: "This is the deeper reason that Montaigne's peasant isn't troubled until the very end, where the Angel of Death, who has always been sitting on his shoulder, extends his wing. Or at least until he is prematurely startled into dumb awareness, like the 'Husbands' in John Cassavetes' fine film. At times like this, when the awareness dawns that has always been blotted out by frenetic, ready-made activity, we see the transmutation of repression redistilled, so to speak, and the fear of death emerges in pure essence." (Becker, *Denial of Death*, 23)

INTRODUCTION

1. Calvin, *Institutes*, 15.

2. Nietzsche, *Antichrist*, 126.

3. Heraclitus, Fragments DK22B80 and DK22B53.

4. Furman, *Views of the Baptists*, 6.

5. The quoted section is paraphrased from the title of the third track from Bob Dylan's 1964 album *The Times They are A-Changin'*.

CHAPTER 1

1. Gandhi, *Essential Gandhi*, 175.

2. Dahlberg and Krug, "Violence," 5.

3. "List of wars by death toll," *Wikipedia*, https://en.wikipedia.org/wiki/List_of_wars_by_death_toll, accessed on 5/16/2016.

4. Hadid, "Syrian Rebels," para. 7.

5. This was a term originally used by British author H.G. Wells to describe World War I, which ended in 1918.

6. Calaprice, *Quotable Einstein*, 173.

7. Hemingway, *Hemingway on War*, 304.

8. Takakura, "Hibakusha Stories," 14.

9. *The Decision to Drop the Bomb.*

10. Shoah is another term for "holocaust" and in Hebrew translates to "catastrophe." Every year, Israel commemorates this tragedy in a day called "Yom ha-Shoah."

11. Connolly, "Tales from Auschwitz," Sec. 5, para. 11–13.

12. Greene, "Interactive Map," para. 9.

13. McNeil, "The Human Meaning," para. 1.

14. Holmes-Pearson, "A Trail of 4,000 Tears," para. 1.

15. Dominic Moes, email message to author, December 27, 2015.

16. Messer, "Conflict as a Cause of Hunger," para. 7–8.

17. Leaning, "War and the Environment," 5.

18. Ibid.

19. Long, "Post-Paris," 208–9.

20. Devereux, "Famine," 6.

21. Ibid.

22. Messer, "Conflict as a Cause of Hunger," para. 34.

23. The former Secretary of State, Madeleine Albright, when asked if the objectives of the US foreign policy were worth the deaths of roughly half a million Arab children, stated: "I think this is a hard choice, but the price, we think the price is worth it." (From a May 12, 1996 interview with *60 Minutes*)

24. Leaning, "War and the Environment," 8.

25. Sadiq, *Gulf War Aftermath*, 186.

26. Bobichand, "Understanding Violence," para. 7.

27. Pilgrim, "What was Jim Crow," para. 7.

28. Knafo, "When it Comes to Illegal Drug Use," para. 6.

29. Ibid., para. 1.

30. McWhorter, "The War on Drugs," 4–5.

31. Sanchez, "Police Link Brothers," para. 8–10.

32. Robert Lofgren, email to the author, August 7, 2016.

33. Hill, "10 Highest-Grossing Films."

34. The quote is from a November 15, 2015 sermon by Dr. Robert Jeffress from First Baptist Dallas. The clip, in its entirety, can be found at https://www.youtube.com/watch?v=vvjMUrPUfC4. In the Appendix, I will discuss the supposed "wrath of God."

35. Pulliam-Bailey, "Jerry Falwell Jr.," para. 4–5.

36. Heraclitus, fragments DK22B80 and DK22B53.

CHAPTER 2

1. Rabe, *Desire Found Me*, 36.

2. I follow René Girard in that I generally refer to mimesis as a non-conscious phenomenon, or what Psychologist Scott R. Garrels describes as "below phenomenological awareness," while saving the word imitation for the more conscious aspect of human behavior. (Garrels, "Imitation,

Mirror Neurons, and Mimetic Desire," 81) This will be more evident when I specifically discuss the conscious act of imitating Christ.

3. Darwin, *Origin of Species*, 449.

4. René Girard's middle name is Noël, which means "Christmas" in French.

5. Haven, "Stanford Professor," para. 17.

6. Oughourlian, *Psychopolitics*, 79.

7. Girard discusses interdividual psychology in Book III of *Things Hidden Since the Foundation of the World*.

8. For one instance of this, I will turn to my daughter, who, upon learning that I possessed something (I cannot remember what, and she never actually knew!), yelled to me from across the house, "I want that! What do you have?"

9. Girard, *I See Satan*, 15.

10. Ibid.

11. Figure 1. Mimetic desire in action. Figure by Rafael Polendo.

12. Girard, *I See Satan*, xi.

13. *The Raven ReView* poster, entitled "Mimetic Desire," can be found at https://www.ravenfoundation.org/wp-content/uploads/2016/05/Mimetic-Desire-infograph-p2a-796x1030.png.

14. Oughourlian, "Desire is Mimetic," 44.

15. Ibid.

16. Hardin, *Jesus Driven Life*, 143.

17. "Scrap" is a derogatory term Norteños use to describe Sureños.

18. Girard, *Violence and the Sacred*, 79.

19. Figure 2. The violence of all against all vs. all against one. Figure by Rafael Polendo.

20. See "I Desire, You Desire, We Desire," earlier in this chapter for how this cycle repeats.

21. Take a look at how the United States' presidential elections have gone. Because the leader of the nation is such an easy target (and thus, so too is their political party affiliation), the US has nearly alternated

political parties for more than half a century. The list goes: Truman (D), Eisenhower (R), Kennedy/Johnson (D), Nixon/Ford (R), Carter (D), Reagan (R), Bush (R), Clinton (D), Bush (R), Obama (D).

22. Long, "Japanese Incarceration," para. 2.

23. *Habeas corpus* is a recourse in law that attempts to ensure people are imprisoned lawfully.

24. Long, "Japanese Incarceration," para. 2.

25. Navarro, "A Critical Comparison," para. 61.

26. Narayanaswami, "Analysis of Nazi Propaganda," 3–4.

27. I wrote an article entitled "American Christianity's Great Scapegoat (Part I)" for *The Raven ReView* in July, 2015 where I discuss this. That article can be found here: https://www.ravenfoundation.org/american-christianitys-great-scapegoat-part-i/.

28. Tashman, "Pat Robertson: Gay Marriage," para. 1.

29. Ibid., para. 3.

30. Ibid., para. 1.

31. Brian Cordova, email to the author, April 2, 2016.

32. O'Connor, "Gun-Toting Islamophobic Group," para. 7.

33. Ibid., para. 2.

34. Rios, "Vandalized Mosques," para. 3.

35. Del Real, "'Rabid' dogs and closing mosques," para. 7.

36. According to Liz Goodwin's article, "Obama administration defends its Syrian refugee screening," this statement is false. Goodwin writes: "Of the about 2,000 refugees from Syria so far, about half are children, and another quarter are adults over sixty. Texas, California and Michigan have received the greatest number of Syrian refugees, more than 200 migrants in each state. According to a senior administration official, only two percent of those admitted so far are males of military age who are unattached to families." (Goodwin, "Obama," para. 9)

37. Walker, "Donald Trump," para. 47; 51.

38. Tashman, "Pat Robertson: Islam," para. 3.

39. Distefano, "Domestic Terrorism," para. 6.

40. Hardin, "The Pillars of Culture," para. 12. Hardin notes that the term "originary event" is generative anthropologist Eric Gans' "term for the first truly social act by human beings."

41. Hardin, *Jesus Driven Life*, 153.

42. Girard, *Things Hidden*, 19.

43. Ibid., 20.

44. Ibid., 10.

45. Alison, *Raising Abel*, 22.

46. Ibid.

47. Girard, *Things Hidden*, 23.

48. Pierpaolo and Gifford, "Rethinking the Neolithic Revolution," 280–81.

49. Embedded quote from Schmidt, Klaus. "Animals and a Headless Man at Göbekli Tepe." *Neo-Lithics 2*: 38–40.

50. Pierpaolo and Gifford, "Rethinking the Neolithic Revolution," 282.

51. Hassig, "El sacrificio," 47.

52. See Bultmann, Rudolf. *New Testament and Mythology: And other Basic Writings*. Minneapolis: Fortress, 1984.

53. Girard, *Things Hidden*, 106–7.

54. Lévi-Strauss, *Totemism*, 19.

55. Girard, *Things Hidden*, 106.

56. Bailie, *Violence Unveiled*, 100.

57. Girard, *Things Hidden*, 106.

58. For further study in how the mimetic theory transcends fields of study, I recommend *How We Became Human: Mimetic Theory and the Science of Evolutionary Origins*, from Michigan State University Press. In short, it is a collection of essays with contributors ranging from such fields as evolutionary culture theory, cultural anthropology, archeology, cognitive psychology, ethology, and philosophy.

CHAPTER 3

1. Becker, *Denial of Death*, 11.

2. Liechty, "Biography," para. 2.

3. The *Ernest Becker Foundation's* mission statement can be found at their official website at http://ernestbecker.org/?page_id=26.

4. Halman, "Religion as Immortality Project," para. 3.

5. Becker, *Denial of Death*, 26.

6. Ibid., 69.

7. Ibid., 2.

8. Ibid., 210–52.

9. Ibid., 19–20.

10. See, for instance, Rev 16:16.

11. Arminianism is a system of believe that asserts human beings must freely accept Jesus Christ as their "Lord and Savior" in order to earn salvation. Arminians place emphasis on humankind's freedom of choice, whereas, in contrast, Calvinists place more emphasis on God's sovereignty.

12. Becker, *Denial of Death*, 23.

13. Hughes, "The Denial of Death and the Practice of Dying," para. 5. I will note here that not only is the violence these groups engage in due to death anxiety, but also because of our mimetic nature, as warring people groups are often a mirror of the other.

CHAPTER 4

1. Hamerton-Kelly, *Violent Origins*, 141.

2. The Eastern Orthodox tradition posits that death leads to sin, whereas in the West, sin leads to death. For our purposes, we will focus on the relationship between sin and death, rather than which comes first and which comes second.

3. Beck, *Slavery of Death*, 3.

4. Some of the most infamous passages that fit this description include, but are certainly not limited to, Lev 20:9; 25:44–45; Num 31:17–18; Deut 20; 22:20–21; Ps 137:9; and Ezek 9:5.

5. Distefano, *All Set Free*, 39.

6. In *The Biblical Cosmos*, Robin Parry points out that both Mesopotamian and Egyptian mythology state that creation takes place in a watery, formless sea of sorts. In similar fashion, Genesis 1:2 speaks of God speaking light into a dark, "formless void," while breathing wind "over the face of the waters." (Parry, *Biblical Cosmos*, 28–9)

7. This idea originated from Jewish rabbi Isaac Luria's *Lurianic Kabbalah*.

8. Most scholars attribute the first creation story to *source P* (priestly), while the second is said to be written by *source J* (Yahwist).

9. In addition to the withholding of a tree, there are two other dissimilarities between the narratives that I would like to note. In the second story, instead of the man and woman being made together (as they were in the first), the woman is created as an afterthought. She is even made after "every animal of the field and every bird of the air." (Gen 2:19) Furthermore, if you notice *how* she is created, it is only possible because of the man's ability to give (a rib in this case). This story, unlike the first, is heavily patriarchal. The second difference is the implementation of a marriage ritual in Gen 2:23–24, where a man is commanded to leave his mother and father and cling to his wife. With the advent of prohibition and ritual in the second narrative, we have striking evidence that this is a myth, one that is attempting to tell a specific story.

10. Hardin, *Jesus Driven Life*, 173.

11. Girard, *I See Satan*, 82.

12. See the *Epic of Gilgamesh*, the *Epic of Atra-Hasis*, and the flood of *Deucalion* for other similar tales.

13. Hardin, *Jesus Driven Life*, 176.

14. Nuechterlein, "Genesis 9:8–17," para. 2.

15. Girard, *I See Satan*, 7.

16. Exod 20:13–16.

17. The Hebrew verb *ratsach* can be translated as "murder" or "kill."

18. *Chamad* is the Hebrew word we translate to "covet" in the tenth commandment. However, as Girard notes, "The verb 'covet' suggest that an

uncommon desire is prohibited, a perverse desire reserved for hardened sinners. But the Hebrew term translated as 'covet' means just simply 'desire.'" (Girard, *I See Satan*, 7)

19. Ibid., 9.

20. Ibid., 14.

21. The most difficult thing for me to hear was that this story was an analogy for what took place on the cross. Tim LaHaye horrifyingly writes: "Both Isaac and Jesus had fathers who were prepared to slay them to fulfill a larger purpose. As Abraham was willing to sacrifice his son, so too was God willing to sacrifice his only son." (LaHaye, *Exploring Bible Prophecy*, 19)

22. I guess Ishmael does not count?

23. This is the first mention of the word "love" in the Hebrew Scriptures.

24. Henotheism is the belief in and worship of one god, with the acceptance of the existence of other gods. For more on the subject of Hebrew henotheism, see *The Old Testament* by Keith Beebe and *The Triumph of Elohim*, edited by Diana Edelman. There is also a great article entitled "Hebrew Henotheism" by University of Idaho Professor Emeritus Nicholas F. Gier that can be found at http://www.webpages.uidaho.edu/ngier/henotheism.htm.

25. Gil Bailie contends the very same thing when he writes: "Far more than we moderns generally realize, human sacrifice was a fact of life among the peoples of the ancient Near East in tension with whom Israel first achieved cultural self-definition." (Bailie, *Violence Unveiled*, 140)

26. I will note that two servants also joined Abraham and Isaac on the journey (Gen 22:3).

27. See Num 29:2.

28. See Ps 50:8–15; 51:15–17; 69:30–31; Isa 1:10–15; Jer 6:20; Amos 5:21–24; Mic 6:6–7.

29. Menzie, "NIV remains," para. 2.

30. Hardin, "What I Believe," sec. 2, para. 18.

31. Hardin, *Jesus Driven Life*, 184.

32. "Satan" is a title, not a name. Satan comes from the Hebrew "*ha satan,*" meaning "the accuser." The theology of the writer of Job includes the satan as a part of the "council of gods." He is God's "prosecuting

attorney," pointing the accusatory finger at those in the wrong. Thus, in Job 1:7, when the satan is said to be going "to and fro on the earth, and from walking up and down on it," it is because that is what his job was, to search out others in order to prosecute them.

33. This is the last time the satan plays any role in the book.

34. Hardin, *Jesus Driven Life*, 184.

35. Girard, "Job as Failed Scapegoat," 191.

36. Ericksen, "Deliver Us," 123.

37. Ibid.

38. Hardin, *Jesus Driven Life*, 184.

39. Bartlett, "Isaiah 53," 187.

40. Williams, *The Bible*, 159.

41. Ibid.

42. Bartlett, "Isaiah 53," 194.

43. Ibid., 186.

44. Regarding the use of "my" in verse 8, James G. Williams writes: "To comment further on verses 4–10, 'my people' appears in verse 8, raising the question whether God's voice enters in here or whether, perhaps, God is the speaker in verses 7–10...The objections to God as speaker are two. (1) The divine voice would be referring to himself in the third person in verse 10a ('it was the will of the Lord to bruise him,' RSV). (2) And in 10b the Hebrew text reads a second person singular: 'thou makest his life an offering for sin' (my translation). Most translations turn that into a third person singular, 'when he offers his life.' But if we stay with the Hebrew text, it appears to be the people persona speaking to the God persona." (Williams, *The Bible*, 159–60)

45. I will note that the Hebrew phrase translated to "poured out" can also be translated "laid bare." (Bartlett, "Isaiah 53," 201)

46. Ibid.

47. Williams, *The Bible*, 161.

48. Bartlett, "Isaiah 53," 201.

CHAPTER 5

1. Barth, *Humanity of God*, 47.

2. The Second Temple period lasted from 530 BCE until Rome destroyed Jerusalem and the Temple during the First Jewish-Roman War in 70 CE.

3. Hardin, *Jesus Driven Life*, 38.

4. Take, for instance, a group informally known as the Zealots.

5. Gabriel, "A Brief Introduction to Second Temple Judaism," para. 7.

6. Grabbe, *Second Temple Judaism*, 57.

7. Gabriel, "A Brief Introduction to Second Temple Judaism," para. 8.

8. Ibid.

9. Michael Hardin points out that there was not simply one accepted understanding of the concept of "messiah." He writes: "There was a plurality of messianic expectations in ancient Judaism…Sometimes, as with the Qumran community, there would be two Messianic figures, one priestly, and the other kingly. The Samaritans did not have a royal figure like the Judeans, but believed in the coming of a prophet like Moses figure they called 'Taheb.' Others still perceived Messiah within militaristic categories expecting a mighty warrior." (Hardin, *Jesus Driven Life*, 65)

10. In footnote 32 of chapter 4, I mentioned that *ha satan*, or *devil* in Greek, is a label and not a "person." It is my belief that Jesus, during his forty day venture into the wilderness, conquered his own "satanic potential" rather than a sort of quasi-person with its own metaphysical reality. That is not to say that the devil is not real, because it is. But, as my friend Brad Jersak has said on numerous occasions, "It is worse than you think!" So in this way, what Jesus conquers is much more profound in that he conquered something within his "self," rather than an "other."

11. In Luke 4:22, the phrase "all spoke well of him" is actually from the Greek phrase *kai pantes emartyroun auto*, meaning "all bore witness to him." Translators have decided to interpret the phrase positively (*all spoke well*) rather than negatively (*all spoke ill*). Because they have done this, they have in turn caused Jesus' sarcastic retort—"no prophet is accepted in the prophet's hometown"—to not make any sense. A better interpretation would be for the people's "bearing witness" to be a dative of disadvantage (*all spoke ill*). With this interpretation, it would then make sense for Jesus to declare that "no prophet is accepted in the prophet's hometown" (Luke 4:24). (Hardin, *Jesus Driven Life*, 60–61)

12. In 2 Kgs 5, Naaman's army captures a young Israelite girl and forces her to serve Naaman's wife. The prophet Elisha is later sent to Namaan to cleanse him of his leprosy. He does so by having Naaman wash in the Jordan River seven times.

13. Prior to Jesus coming to Nazareth, Luke 4:14–15 tell us that he had been teaching in Galilee and that he was "praised by everyone." But there is no mention of what he had been teaching.

14. Michael Hardin makes an analogy between Isa 61:1–2 and John 3:16. In essence, the importance of Isa 61:1–2 for Jews is akin to what John 3:16 is for Christians. (Hardin, *Jesus Driven Life*, 60–61)

15. If you think back to chapter 3, you should recall that I discussed how human beings cling (often violently) to our systems of immortality. We do so in order to defend our sense of the heroic "self." For many Jews, the wicked receiving their "just desserts" was a part of their system of belief and thus, to have it challenged was quite a dangerous notion, as any chink in the armor could lead to psychological, spiritual, and physical ruin. That is to say, to have a complete paradigm shift in their theological thinking would be to have everything they had built come tumbling down like a house of cards.

16. Hardin, *Jesus Driven Life*, 63.

17. Ibid.

18. Ibid., 65.

19. I am referring to both the Roman and Jewish authorities.

20. In Luke's version (the Sermon on the Plain), the Father's perfection is described as mercy. Luke 6:36 tells us to "be merciful, just as your Father is merciful."

21. I believe this is what Paul meant in Gal 3:19, which reads: "Why then the law? It was added because of transgressions, until the offspring would come to whom the promise had been made; and it was ordained through angels by a mediator." In fact, the Greek phrase "*ton parabaseon charin prosetethe*" should read "in order to provoke transgressions," rather than "because of transgressions," thus strengthening such an interpretation. Pauline scholar J. Louis Martyn explains why this is a preferred translation: "The term *charin* (the accusative of *charis*, used as a preposition) can indicate either a cause (thus 'because of transgressions') or a goal ('in order to produce or provoke transgressions'). Because the basic meaning of transgression is the breaking of an established and recognized command, Paul surely thinks of the Law as antedating these transgressions and, indeed, very probably as producing

them. If the gospel is now eliciting faith (3:2, 5), the Law entered the picture, in its own time, in order to elicit transgressions (so also Rom 5:20). That is a view of the Law for which there is no proper parallel in Jewish traditions, where the Law is thought to increase resistance to transgressions." (Martyn, *Galatians*, 354–55)

22. Girard, *I See Satan*, 13.

23. Hardin, *Jesus Driven Life*, 34.

24. Ibid., 251–52.

25. In *Desire Found Me*, André Rabe points out: "The real source of evil is the lies we are unconsciously bound by. What drives people to violence (causing suffering), even to murder in the name of God, is the mindset birthed by accusation—the devil. (The devil is the Greek equivalent to the Hebrew *satan*). As such they are captivated by desires and bound to fulfill intentions of which the source is not recognized by them. These 'disciples' are modeling accusation and as such the accuser, better known as the devil." (Rabe, *Desire Found Me*, 206–7)

26. Grayson, "The Cross," sec. 1, para. 4.

27. Scholars have debated and continue to debate the best context for the phrase "the son of man." Some suggest that the best context is Dan 7 and 9, while others opt for Ps 8, Ezekiel, or even the apocryphal book of *1 Enoch* (Hardin, *Jesus Driven Life*, 68).

28. Ibid.

29. Ibid., 69.

30. Girard, "Are the Gospels Mythical?," para. 10.

31. I would like to note how this collective and cyclical violence—just like in Jeremiah's day—indeed comes down upon that very genera-tion roughly forty years later in 70 CE. Those who didn't heed Jesus' warnings—which was nearly everyone—literally ended up in Gehenna (the English word unfortunately translated as "hell"). It is in this valley of slaughter, as it was known (Jer 19:6), where the bodies of those who were massacred in Jerusalem were burned. Prophetically knowing this causes Jesus to lament over Jerusalem and her people (Matt 23:37–39) because, again, they just do not see it coming. They are blind to their own sacrificial violence that will lead to their ruin, whereupon the altar the blood of the prophets continues to be shed. And it has been this way since the death of Abel; that is to say, since the foundation of the world (i.e., human civilization. See Gen 4:17).

32. Hardin, *Jesus Driven Life*, 105. See 2 Chron 24:20–21.

33. See, also, 1 Peter 1:20.

34. John 12:15 is an echo from Zech 9:9–10, which reads: "Rejoice greatly, O daughter Zion! Shout aloud, O daughter Jerusalem! Lo, your king comes to you; triumphant and victorious is he, humble and riding on a donkey. He will cut off the chariot from Ephraim and the war-horse from Jerusalem; and the battle bow shall be cut off, and he shall command peace to the nations; his dominion shall be from sea to sea, and from the River to the ends of the earth."

35. Hardin, *Jesus Driven Life*, 105.

36. Ibid., 104.

37. This word of forgiveness that Jesus speaks makes his story different than that of the Suffering Servant of Isaiah. If you recall, that figure is silent during his violent slaying. Jesus, however, is not. He offers forgiveness to the very ones putting him through such a dehumanizing event.

38. Later, in Acts 3:17, Peter reaffirms the ignorance of those who murder Jesus when he states: "And now, friends, I know that you acted in ignorance, as did also your rulers." Of this ignorance that both Jesus and Peter affirm, Girard writes: "Persecutors think they are doing good, the right thing; they believe they are working for justice and truth; they believe they are saving the community" (Girard, *I See Satan*, 126)

39. Alison, *Raising Abel*, 27.

40. Holy Saturday celebrates not only the day Jesus is laid to rest in the tomb, but, especially in Eastern Orthodoxy, the day Jesus raises those who had been trapped in *Hades*. This is known as "The Harrowing of Hades."

41. Bailie, *Violence Unveiled*, 33.

42. See Euripides, *The Bacchae and Other Plays*. New York; Penguin, 1954.

CHAPTER 6

1. Alison, *Knowing Jesus*, 33.

2. For one such example, in Greek mythology, it is said that after Zeus' son Dionysus is torn apart, boiled, and then eaten by a group of Titans, Zeus hurls his infamous thunderbolt and destroys the Titans. Dionysus' grandmother Rhea then uses their ashes to bring Dionysus back to life.

3. The Sadducees, for instance, did not believe in a Resurrection of the dead, whereas the Pharisees did.

4. Wright, *Surprised by Scripture*, 47.

5. Ibid.

6. Ibid., 48.

7. Ibid.

8. Ibid.

9. Ibid., 49.

10. Ibid.

11. I will note that the point of the phrase "if you retain the sins of any, they are retained" isn't to actually refrain from forgiving others, but rather, that we can choose to follow Jesus (or not) in forgiving sins in the same way he did (even while hanging from a cross).

12. Hegesippus, "Fragments from the Acts of the Church," para. 5.

13. Pamphilius, *Church History*, 175.

14. It is after Roman Emperor Nero accuses Christians of being responsible for a fire that happened in Rome during the first century, when Christians become even easier targets, as they were often arrested and murdered for, as Kenneth D. Whitehead puts it: "simply being Christians." (Whitehead, "Witnesses," para. 1)

15. Ibid., para. 11.

16. Pamphilius, *Church History,* 331.

17. Hardin, *Jesus Driven Life*, 51.

18. This is why many early Christians worked toward memorizing what is called *The Didache*. Like the Sermon on the Mount, this piece of literature emphasizes such teachings as "bless those who curse you," "pray for your enemies," and "turn the other cheek." (Hoole, "Didache," 75)

19. Hardin, *Jesus Driven Life*, 38.

20. In the Appendix, I will discuss how Paul does this same type of thing in his letter to the Romans.

CHAPTER 7

1. These quotes, along with many others from the early church fathers, can be found at http://www.tentmaker.org/Quotes/churchfathersquotes.htm.

2. Hardin, "Romans 5:12–21," 2.

3. Talbott, *Inescapable Love of God*, 58.

4. Ibid.

5. See, for instance, Eph 2:3. Now, I will note that while Paul may not have written Ephesians, it does represent Pauline thought.

6. Talbott, *Inescapable Love of God*, 70.

7. Ibid., 61.

8. This letter is number nine in a collection entitled *A Journey with Two Mystics: Conversations between a Girardian and a Wattsian* (Release date TBD).

9. I will note that the Bible never actually states that someone must have a "personal relationship with Jesus" in order to achieve salvation.

10. Kierkegaard, *Journals and Papers*, 557.

CHAPTER 8

1. Polanyi, *Tacit Dimension*, 4.

2. Muhaiyaddeen, *God's Psychology*, 181.

3. See, for instance, Mark 1:15, Matt 3:2; 4:17.

4. Glueck, "Cruz Pledges," para. 2.

APPENDIX

1. Quote from a January 10, 2014 Tweet by Mark Driscoll that can be found here: https://twitter.com/PastorMark/status/421674123132416000.

2. Wilkinson, "Did Jesus Speak," para. 1–4.

3. Ibid.

4. See, also, 2 Chron 28:3.

5. Jersak, "Salted with Fire," para. 6.

6. Ibid., para 12.

7. From a June 29, 2016 Facebook post by Jeff Turner—found at https://www.facebook.com/SoundOfAwakening/posts/10206813626484149.

8. Barclay, *Spiritual Autobiography*, 66.

9. Talbott, *Inescapable Love of God*, 83–84.

10. Ibid., 89–90.

11. Original quote from Enns, "Apostolic Hermeneutics," 277, sourced from Jersak, "I Saw a Lamb," 316.

12. This quote comes from an interview Driscoll, along with six other Christian faith leaders, did with *Relevant Magazine*. The quote, in its entirety, can be found here: http://web.archive.org/web/20071013102203/http://relevantmagazine.com/god_article.php?id=7418.

13. Jersak, "I Saw a Lamb," 330.

14. MacDonald, *Evangelical Universalist*, 123–27.

15. Jersak, "I Saw a Lamb," 328.

16. Wright, *Justification*, 21.

17. Edwards, "The Works," 458.

18. The word Driscoll is looking for is "meritorious."

19. A clip of Driscoll's infamous sermon can be found at https://www.youtube.com/watch?v=uSml8m8ZAdk.

20. Campbell, *Deliverance of God*, 495–518.

21. In reality, he would have sent a reader—Phoebe (Rom 16:1).

22. Ibid., 587.

23. Regarding the order of Paul's letters, Pauline scholar J. Louis Martyn states: "Galatians thus antedates all of the Corinthian letters, and Romans comes after them." (Martyn, *Galatians*, 20)

24. Much of this rhetoric comes from "Wisdom of Solomon," chapters 13–14 most specifically.

25. For those interested, my friend and fellow Girardian Paul Nuechterlein has a rendering of Romans 1:1–4:3 in dialog form that can be found at http://girardianlectionary.net/special_series/Romans1-3_read-in-light-of-Campbell.htm.

26. Nuechterlein, "My Core Convictions," part 2.

BIBLIOGRAPHY

Alison, James. *Knowing Jesus*. Springfield: Templegate, 1993.

———. *Raising Abel: The Recovery of the Eschatological Imagination*. New York: Crossroad, 1996.

Antonello, Pierpaolo and Gifford, Paul. "Rethinking the Neolithic Revolution: Symbolism and Sacrifice at Göbekli Tepe." In *How we Became Human: Mimetic Theory and the Science of Evolutionary Origins*. Edited by Pierpaolo and Gifford. East Lansing: Michigan State University Press, 2015.

Bailie, Gil. *Violence Unveiled: Humanity at the Crossroads*. St. Louis: Crossroad, 1996.

Barclay, William. *A Spiritual Autobiography*. Grand Rapids: Eerdmans, 1977.

Barth, Karl. *The Humanity of God*. Louisville: Westminster John Knox Press, 1960.

Bartlett, Anthony. "Isaiah 53." In *The Jesus Driven Life: Reconnecting Humanity with Jesus*. Lancaster: JDL, 2010.

Beck, Richard. *The Slavery of Death*. Eugene: Cascade, 2013.

Becker, Ernest. *The Denial of Death*. New York: Free Press, 1973.

Bobichand, Rajkumar. "Understanding Violence Triangle and Structural Violence." Manipur: Imphal, 2012. http://kanglaonline.com/2012/07/understanding-violence-triangle-and-structural-violence-by-rajkumar-bobichand/.

Campbell, Douglas. *The Deliverance of God: An Apocalyptic Rereading of Justification in Paul*. Grand Rapids: Eerdmans, 2013.

Calaprice, Alice. *The New Quotable Einstein*. Princeton: Princeton University Press, 2005.

Connolly, Kate. "Tales from Auschwitz: Survivor Stories." http://www.theguardian.com/world/2015/jan/26/tales-from-auschwitz-survivor-stories.

Dahlberg, Linda L., and Krug, Etienne G. "Violence—a global public health problem." In *World Report on Violence and Health*, edited by Etienne G. Krug et al. Geneva: World Health Organization, 2002.

Del Real, Jose A., Fahrenthold, David A. "'Rabid' dogs and closing mosques: Anti-Islam rhetoric grows in GOP." *Washington Post* (November 2015). https://www.washingtonpost.com/politics/rabid-dogs-and-muslim-id-cards-anti-islam-rhetoric-grows-in-gop/2015/11/19/1cdf9f04-8ee5-11e5-baf4-bdf37355da0c_story.html.

Darwin, Charles. *On the Origin of Species*. New York: Modern Library, 1859.

Devereux, Stephen. "Famine in the Twentieth Century." https://www.ids.ac.uk/files/dmfile/wp105.pdf.

Distefano, Matthew J. *All Set Free: How God is Revealed in Jesus and Why that is Really Good News*. Eugene: Resource, 2015.

———. "Domestic Terrorism: My take on the Militia Takeover of a Federal Building in Oregon." *The Raven ReView* (January 2016). https://www.ravenfoundation.org/domestic-terrorism-my-take-on-the-militia-takeover-of-a-federal-building-in-oregon/.

———. "Paul's Inclusive Theology: A Consistent View Throughout the Pauline Corpus." *Preaching Peace* (2016). http://www.preachingpeace.org/teaching-resources/articles/25-articles-ebooks/articles-by-friends-of-preaching-peace/335-paul%E2%80%80%99s-inclusive-theology-a-consistent-view-throughout-the-pauline-corpus.html.

Edwards, Jonathan. *The Works of President Edwards*. New York: Burt Franklin, 1968.

Enns, Peter. "Apostolic Hermeneutics and an Evangelical Doctrine of Scripture: Moving Beyond a Modernist Impasse." *Westminster Theological Journal* 65 (2003) 277.

Ericksen, Adam. "Deliver Us From Evil." In *All Set Free: How God is Revealed in Jesus and Why That is Really Good News*. Eugene: Resource, 2015.

Furman, Richard. "Exposition of the Views of the Baptists, Relative to the Colored Population in the United States: In Communication to the Governor of South Carolina." Second ed. Charleston, 1838. http://eweb.furman.edu/~benson/docs/rcd-fmn1.htm.

Gabriel, Vincent. "A Brief Introduction to Second Temple Judaism." *On Behalf of All* (March 2013). https://blogs.ancientfaith.com/onbehalfofall/a-brief-introduction-to-second-temple-judaism/.

Gandhi, Mahatma. *The Essential Gandhi: An Anthology of His Writings on His Life, Work, and Ideas*. New York: Vintage, 2002.

Garrels, Scott R. "Imitation, Mirror Neurons, and Mimetic Desire: Convergence between the Mimetic Theory of René Girard and Empirical Research on Imitation." *Contagion: Journal of Violence, Mimesis, and Culture* 12–13 (2006) 47–86. http://static1.squarespace.com/static/55a55b50e4b08015467323fc/t/565f4a92e4b0a6f556b4e7c4/1449085586674/Contagion_12-13_Garrels_47-86.pdf.

Girard, René. "Are the Gospels Mythical?" *First Things* (April 1996). http://www.firstthings.com/article/1996/04/002-are-the-gospels-mythical.

———. *I See Satan Fall Like Lightning*. Translated by James G. Williams. New York: Orbis, 2001.

———. "Job as Failed Scapegoat" In *The Voice from the Whirlwind: Interpreting the Book of Job*. Edited by Leo G. Perdue and W. Clark Gilpin. Nashville: Abingdon, 1992.

———. *Things Hidden Since the Foundation of the World*. Translated by Bann, Stephen and Metteer, Michael. Stanford: Stanford University Press, 1978.

———. *Violence and the Sacred*. Translated by Patrick Gregory. Baltimore: Johns Hopkins University Press, 1979.

Glueck, Katie. "Cruz pledges relentless bombing to destroy ISIL." *Politico* (December 2015). http://www.politico.com/story/2015/12/cruz-isil-bombing-216454.

Goodwin, Liz. "Obama administration defends its Syrian refugee screening." *Yahoo! Politics* (November 2015). https://www.yahoo.com/politics/obama-administration-defends-its-syrian-refugee-212248421.html.

Grabbe, Lester. *An Introduction to Second Temple Judaism: History and Religion of the Jews in the Time of Nehemiah, the Maccabees, Hillel, and Jesus*. New York: T&T Clark, 2010.

Grayson, Rob. "The Cross: Religious Self-Projection or Radical Discontinuity?" *Faith Meets World* (February 2016). http://www.faithmeetsworld.com/the-cross-religious-self-projection-or-radical-discontinuity/.

Greene, Richard Allen, and Torre, Inez. "Interactive Map: Nazi Death Camps." *CNN* (April 2015). http://www.cnn.com/2015/01/26/world/nazi-death-camps/.

Hadid, Diaa. "Syrian Rebels and Government Reach Truce in Besieged Area." *Huffington Post* (January 2015). http://www.huffingtonpost.com/2015/01/15/syria-rebel-truce_n_6478226.html?ncid=txtlnkusaolp00000592.

Halman, Talat. "Religion as Immortality Project: An Anthropological Perspective at the Heart of the Study of Religion." (2009). http://www.halmantle.com/2009/05/religion-as-immortality-project.html.

Hamerton-Kelly, Robert, ed. *Violent Origins: Ritual Killing and Cultural Foundation*. Stanford: Stanford University Press, 1987.

Hardin, Michael. *The Jesus Driven Life: Reconnecting Humanity with Jesus*. Lancaster: JDL, 2010.

―――. "The Pillars of Culture: Prohibition, Ritual, and Myth." *Preaching Peace*. http://www.preachingpeace.org/teaching-resources/articles/23-articles-ebooks/introductory-articles/55-the-pillars-of-culture-prohibition-ritual-and-myth.html.

―――. "Romans 5:12–21: An Exegesis by Michael Hardin." Lancaster: JDL, 2015.

―――. "What I Believe: Expositions on the Nicene Creed for Christians in the Twenty-First Century." Lancaster: JDL, 2013. http://www.preachingpeace.org/26-articles-ebooks/articles-ebooks-by-michael-hardin/77-what-i-believe-expositions-on-the-nicene-creed.html.

Hartley, John E. *The Book of Job*. Grand Rapids: Eerdmans, 1988.

Hassig, Ross. "El Sacrificio y las guerras floridas." *Arqueología Mexicana* XI (2003).

Haven, Cynthia. "Stanford Professor and Eminent French Theorist René Girard, member of the Académie Française, dies at 91." *Stanford News* (November 2015). http://news.stanford.edu/news/2015/november/rene-girard-obit-110415.html.

Hegesippus, "The Acts of the Church; Concerning the Martyrdom of James, the Brother of the Lord, Book V." http://www.earlychristianwritings.com/text/hegesippus.html.

Hemingway, Ernest. *Hemingway on War*. New York: Scribner, 2003.

Hill, Michelle. "10 Highest-Grossing Films of 2015." http://www.upi.com/Entertainment_News/Movies/2015/12/23/10-highest-grossing-films-of-2015/3501449671372/.

Holmes-Pearson, Ellen. "A Trail of 4,000 Tears." http://teachinghistory.org/history-content/ask-a-historian/25652.

Hoole, Charles H. "The Didache." Translated by Charles H. Hoole. London: David Nutt, 1894. http://www.sacred-texts.com/chr/did/index.htm.

Hughes, Glenn. "The Denial of Death and the Practice of Dying." *Ernest Becker Foundation* (2015). http://ernestbecker.org/?page_id=989.

Jersak, Bradley. *Her Gates will Never be Shut: Hell, Hope, and the New Jerusalem.* Eugene: Wipf & Stock, 2009.

———. "I Saw a Lamb," In *The Jesus Driven Life: Reconnecting Humanity with Jesus.* 2nd Ed. Lancaster: JDL, 2013.

———. "Salted with Fire." *Christianity Without the Religion* (February 2016). http://christianity-without-the-religion.blogspot.com/2016/02/q-self-amputation-hellfire-mark-9-brad.html.

———. "The so-called 'violence' of Jesus in the so-called 'cleansing of the temple.'" *Clarion: Journal of Spirituality and Justice* (June 2013). http://www.clarion-journal.com/clarion_journal_of_spirit/2013/06/the-so-called-violence-of-jesus-in-the-so-called-cleansing-of-the-temple-by-brad-jersak.html.

Kierkegaard, Søren. *Journals and Papers: Volume 6, Autobiographical, Part Two, 1848–1855.* Edited and Translated by Howard V. Hong and Edna H. Hong. Bloomington: Indiana University Press, 1978.

———. *Selections from the Writings of Kierkegaard.* Translated by Lee M. Hollander. New York: Anchor, 1960.

Knafo, Saki. "When it Comes to Illegal Drug Use, White America Does the Crime, Black America Gets the Time." *Huffington Post* (September 2013). http://www.huffingtonpost.com/2013/09/17/racial-disparity-drug-use_n_3941346.html.

LaHaye, Tim and Hindson, Ed, eds. *Exploring Bible Prophecy: From Genesis to Revelation: Clarifying the Meaning of Every Prophetic Passage.* Eugene: Harvest House, 2006.

Leaning, Jennifer. "War and the Environment: Human Health Consequences of the Environmental Damage of War." https://mitpress.mit.edu/sites/default/files/titles/content/9780262531184_sch_0001.pdf.

Lee, John. "Japanese Incarceration–Executive Order 9066 (1942)." http://www.dartmouth.edu/~hist32/History/S16%20-%20Japanese%20Incarceration%20-%20Executive%20Order%209066%20(1942).htm.

Lévi-Strauss, Claude. *Totemism.* Boston: Beacon, 1963.

Liechty, Daniel. "Biography." *Ernest Becker Foundation* (2015). http://ernestbecker.org/new/?page_id=121.

———. "Sixteen Central Ideas of the Theory of Generative Death Anxiety." *Ernest Becker Foundation.* http://ernestbecker.org/?page_id=991.

Long, Ngo Vinh. "Post-Paris Agreement Struggles and the Fall of Saigon." In *The Vietnam War: Vietnamese and American Perspectives.* Edited by Jayne S. Werner and Luu Doan Huynh. Armonk: M.E. Sharpe, 1993.

MacDonald, Gregory. *The Evangelical Universalist.* Eugene: Cascade, 2012.

Martyn, J. Louis. *Galatians: A New Translation with Introduction and Commentary.* New Haven: Yale University Press, 1997.

McNeil, Sara. "The Human Meaning of Removal." *Digital History* (2016). http://www.digitalhistory.uh.edu/active_learning/explorations/indian_removal/watts.cfm.

McWhorter, John. "How the War on Drugs is Destroying Black America." *Cato's Letter.* Volume 9, Number 1 (2011) 1–5. http://object.cato.org/sites/cato.org/files/pubs/pdf/catosletterv9n1.pdf.

Menzie, Nicola. "NIV remains the bestselling Bible translation." *Christian Today* (March 2013). http://www.christiantoday.com.au/article/niv.remains.the.bestselling.bible.translation/15171.htm.

Messer, Ellen, et al. "Conflict as a Cause of Hunger." In *Who's Hungry? And How do we Know? Food Shortage, Poverty, and Deprivation.* New York: United Nations University Press, 1998.

Muhaiyaddeen, Bawa. *God's Psychology: A Sufi Explanation.* Philadelphia: Fellowship, 2007.

Narayanaswami, Karthik. "Analysis of Nazi Propaganda." http://blogs.harvard.edu/karthik/files/2011/04/HIST-1572-Analysis-of-Nazi-Propaganda-KNarayanaswami.pdf.

Navarro, Anthony V. "A Critical Comparison between Japanese and American Propaganda during World War II." https://www.msu.edu/~navarro6/srop.html.

Nietzsche, Friedrich. *The Antichrist.* New York: Alfred A. Knopf, 1920.

Nuechterlein, Paul. "My Core Convictions: Nonviolence and the Christian Faith." *Girardian Lectionary* (February 2012). http://girardianlectionary.net/core_convictions.htm.

O'Connor, Lydia. "Gun-Toting Islamophobic Group Protests Outside Texas Mosque." *Huffington Post* (November 2015). http://www.huffingtonpost.com/entry/irving-texas-armed-mosque-protest_5651eddfe4b0d4093a581d14.

Oughourlian, Jean-Michel. "Desire is Mimetic: A Clinical Approach." *Contagion: Journal of Violence, Mimesis, and Culture* 3 (1996) 43–49. http://www.uibk.ac.at/theol/cover/contagion/contagion3/contagion03_oughourlian.pdf.

———. *Psychopolitics: Conversations with Trevor Cribben Merrill.* East Lansing: Michigan State University Press, 2012.

———. *The Puppet of Desire: The Psychology of Hysteria, Possession, and Hypnosis.* Translated by Eugene Webb. Stanford: Stanford University Press, 2001.

Pamphilius, Eusebius. *Church History, Life of Constantine, Oration in praise of Constantine.* Translated by Arthur Cushman. New York: Christian Literature, 1890.

Parry, Robin. *The Biblical Cosmos: A Pilgrim's Guide to the Weird and Wonderful World of the Bible.* Eugene: Cascade, 2014.

Peterson, Robert A. *Hell on Trial: The Case for Eternal Punishment.* Phillipsburg: P&R, 1995.

Pilgrim, David. "What was Jim Crow?" http://www.ferris.edu/jimcrow/what.htm.

Plato. *Protagoras.* Library of Liberal Arts. Edited by Gregory Vlastos. Translated by Benjamin Jowett and Martin Oswald. New York: Bobbs-Merrill, 1956.

Polanyi, Michael. *The Tacit Dimension.* Chicago: University of Chicago Press, 1966.

Pratt, Jason. "Christian Universalism: An Exegetical Compilation." *Evangelical Universalism* (August 2014). http://evangelicaluniversalist.com/forum/viewtopic.php?f=12&t=5827.

Pulliam-Bailey, Sarah. "Jerry Falwell Jr.: 'If more good people had concealed-carry permits, then we could end those' Islamist terrorists." *Washington Post* (December 2015). https://www.washingtonpost.com/news/acts-of-faith/wp/2015/12/05/liberty-university-president-if-more-good-people-had-concealed-guns-we-could-end-those-muslims/.

Rabe, André. *Desire Found Me.* André Rabe: 2015.

Rios, Edwin. "Vandalized Mosques, Threats of Violence—Anti-Muslim Hate Crimes on the Rise." *Mother Jones* (November 2015). http://www.motherjones.com/mojo/2015/11/anti-muslim-hate-crimes-rise.

Sadiq, Muhammad and McCain, John Charles. *The Gulf War Aftermath: An Environmental Tragedy.* Berlin: Springer, 1993.

Sanchez, Rene. "Police Link Brothers to Christian Identity." *Washington Post* (July 1999). http://www.washingtonpost.com/wp-srv/national/longterm/hatecrimes/stories/brothers072199.htm.

Takakura, Akiko. "Hibakusha Stories." In *The Story of Hiroshima*. http://www.hiroshima-remembered.com/history/hiroshima/page14.html.

Talbott, Thomas. *The Inescapable Love of God*. Second ed. Eugene: Cascade, 2014.

Tashman, Brian. "Pat Robertson: Gay Marriage Will Lead to God's Wrath, Turn US into Sodom." http://www.rightwingwatch.org/content/pat-robertson-gay-marriage-will-lead-gods-wrath-turn-us-sodom.

———. "Pat Robertson: Islam is Not a Religion But a Military Group 'Bent on World Domination.'" http://www.rightwingwatch.org/content/pat-robertson-islam-not-religion-military-group-bent-world-domination.

The Decision to Drop the Bomb, DVD. Produced by Freed, Fred, and Giovannitti, Len. Wilmette: Films, Inc., 1965.

Walker, Hunter. "Donald Trump has big plans for 'radical Islamic' terrorists, 2016 and 'that communist' Bernie Sanders." *Yahoo! Politics* (November 2015). https://www.yahoo.com/politics/donald-trump-has-big-plans-1303117537878070.html.

Whitehead, Kenneth D. "Witnesses of the Passion." *Touchstone: A Journal of Mere Christianity* 17, no. 5 (2004). http://www.touchstonemag.com/archives/article.php?id=17-05-023-f. ·

Wilkinson, Dan. "Did Jesus speak more about Hell than about Heaven?" *Unfundamentalist Christians* (January 2015). http://www.patheos.com/blogs/unfundamentalistchristians/2015/01/did-jesus-speak-more-about-hell-than-about-heaven/.

Williams, James G. *The Bible, Violence, and the Sacred: Liberation from the Myth of Sanctioned Violence*. San Francisco: Harper Collins, 1991.

Wright, N.T. *Justification: God's Plan and Paul's Vision*. Westmont: IVP Academic, 2009.

———. *Surprised by Hope: Rethinking Heaven, the Resurrection, and the Mission of the Church*. New York: HarperOne, 2008.

———. *Surprised by Scripture: Engaging Contemporary Issues*. New York: HarperOne, 2014.

For more information about Matthew J. Distefano
or to contact him for speaking engagements,
please visit *www.allsetfree.com*

 **QUOIR**

Many voices. One message.

Quoir is a boutique publishing company
with a single message: Christ is all.
Our books explore both His
cosmic nature and corporate expression.

For more information, please visit
www.quoir.com